NAT GAS MILLION$

NAT GAS MILLION$

Insider Secrets To Striking It Rich

Jay Bhatty, CFA

Copyright © 2024 by Jay Bhatty

All rights reserved. No part of this book may be used or reproduced in any manner whatsoever without prior written consent of the author, except as provided by the United States of America copyright laws.

Published by Best Seller Publishing©, St. Augustine, FL
Best Seller Publishing© is a registered trademark.
Printed in the United States of America.

ISBN: 978-1-962595-58-2

This publication is designed to provide accurate and authoritative information with regard to the subject matter covered. It is sold with the understanding that the publisher is not engaged in rendering legal, accounting, or other professional advice. If legal advice or other expert assistance is required, the services of a competent professional should be sought. The opinions expressed by the author in this book are not endorsed by Best Seller Publishing© and are the sole responsibility of the author rendering this opinion.

For more information, please write:
Best Seller Publishing, Inc.
53 Marine Street
St. Augustine, FL 32084
Or call 1 (626) 765-9750
Visit us online at: www.BestSellerPublishing.org

Table of Contents

Preface 1

Foreword: Fletcher Sturm 3

Introduction: An Insider's Guide to Accumulating
Wealth in the Nat Gas Industry 5

Natural Gas: The Most Important Commodity of Our Lives 11

Introduction for Nat Gas Traders... 15

Types of Instruments Traded 17

Three Equations Every Trader Must Know 21

Valuing and Trading Gas Storage.. 43

Valuing and Trading Gas Transport... 63

Valuing and Trading a Gas Park or Loan.. 81

Ten for Ten: Ten Trading Strategies to Make You
$10 Million per Year.. 95

Introduction for Nat Gas Schedulers... 131

Schedulers Who Aspire to Be Traders.. 139

The Four Nomination Models Every Scheduler
Must Know 145

Cracking the Code on Pipeline Tariffs 157

Introduction for Nat Gas Technologists 167

Where to Implement AI in Your Organization 169

RPA: Welcome to the Age of Digital Labor 173

The Top Five Traits of High Earners in the Nat Gas Industry 177

Bonus: How to Come Up with Your Money-Making
Business Idea 185

Conclusion 191

Afterword 195

Index 197

References 199

Advanced Praise

"Jay has successfully illustrated the key concepts in natural gas trading, utilizing technical analysis and historical relevance, and has presented a detailed overview of the physical gas business to ensure customers, utilities, and power plants receive their gas. My interns will be assigned this book for reference."

—**JEFF LOWNEY**, Director US Origination and Business Development, Uniper

"Jay's multifaceted experience as a scheduler, trader, technologist, and entrepreneur provides an exceptional foundation for this much-needed resource. His deep understanding of the natural gas trading world and the intricacies of this fast-paced industry make this book an invaluable read."

—**TAMMY NORMAN**, President & COO, Mansfield Power & Gas

"This book is an indispensable resource for anyone serious about launching or propelling their career in the natural gas industry. It offers not just valuable and practical guidance, but a masterclass in the skills and knowledge needed for excelling in this competitive field."

—**DILANKA SEIMON**, Chief Commercial Officer, Enlink Midstream

"A must-read guide for both newcomers and experienced professionals, offering a thorough overview of natural gas trading and logistics, enriched with insights on leveraging technology and industry-leading strategies."

—**LEE NORRIS**, Chief Information Officer, Symmetry Energy Solutions

"*Indispensable must-read for anyone aiming to build a thriving career in the natural gas industry. Contains a fascinating chapter that addresses leveraging Artificial Intelligence and Robotic Process Automation to enhance productivity.*"

—**BRIAN RHODES**, Director, Asset Management and Origination, ConocoPhillips

"*This book demonstrates how data-driven insights and practical wisdom can optimize and elevate your trading prowess. Nat Gas Millions is a must-read for industry professionals seeking to transform their career.*"

—**T.C. GRAY**, Vice President, ARM Energy

"*Nat Gas Millions is a must-read for everyone in the natural gas industry. The book weaves together cutting-edge strategies and insights on trading, scheduling, risk management, and technology, making it an invaluable resource for both beginners and seasoned professionals.*"

—**NEEL PINGE**, Chief Risk Officer, Commercial Bank of California

"*Nat Gas Millions takes you on a journey into the business of natural gas and breaks down the complex concepts of the industry in a manner which is comprehensive yet accessible. It's a must read for anyone in the Natural Gas Industry.*"

—**CARIE FYE**, Scheduling Manger, Symmetry Energy

"*This is essential reading for anyone entering the energy trading industry. While the fundamentals described in it are important for U.S. natural gas, the underlying concepts are similar for any commodity. We're planning to make it an important part of our training and continuing education efforts.*"

—**SAMEER SOLEJA**, Founder & CEO, Molecule Software

Acknowledgements

Writing this book has been a journey, and I could not have completed it without the support of many wonderful people.

My heartfelt thanks go to my editor, Bob Harpole, whose insightful feedback and keen eye for detail were invaluable.

Thank you to the invaluable input from the 53 natural gas traders, 32 natural gas schedulers, and 12 chief technology officers at natural gas trading companies whom I interviewed extensively during the writing of this book and who entertained my probing questions on the secrets to their career successes and failures. This book represents the collective knowledge of these professionals who worked at natural gas trading companies, including JPMorgan, Macquarie, Hartree, TC Energy, Vistra, Exxon, Williams, EDF, Constellation, Symmetry, Tenaska, EQT, Duke, Shell, BP, Intercontinental Exchange, Chevron, Conoco, Gas South, Vitol, Mercuria, Koch, J Aron, NJR, and Canadian Natural Resources. In their careers, they have witnessed major industry milestones, from the establishment of the Henry Hub benchmark in the late 1990s to the expansion of LNG in the 2000s, the shale gas boom starting in 2008, the growing share of natural gas vis-à-vis coal starting in 2010, the COVID-19 pandemic in 2020, the Ukraine crisis in 2022, and the advent of AI starting in 2023. My hope in writing this book is that their experiences will help shape the views of natural gas traders, schedulers, and technologists over the next 50 years, enabling them to attain immense profitability for their companies as well as accumulate wealth in their personal careers.

Special thanks to Keith Cooper (natural gas trader at TC Energy Marketing) and Ahmed Saeed (former natural gas trader at Macquarie & Koch), whose knowledge on the topic was a crucial resource.

Lastly, I want to acknowledge my family, friends, and readers who offered their time and feedback on early drafts. Your encouragement and suggestions have been essential in shaping this book into its final form. Thank you all for being part of this journey with me.

Dedication

To my mentors in the natural gas industry, whose guidance and wisdom illuminated my path: Your patience in teaching me the foundational concepts, your encouragement in applying them to trading, and your willingness to let me make mistakes and learn from them have been truly invaluable. This book is a testament to your enduring support and belief in my potential. Thank you for shaping my journey and for the knowledge that has fueled my growth.

DISCLAIMER

The information contained in this book is for informational purposes only. While the author has made every effort to ensure the accuracy and completeness of the information provided, the author and publisher assume no responsibility for errors, inaccuracies, omissions, or any other inconsistencies herein. This book is not intended to replace professional advice, whether legal, financial, or otherwise. Readers are encouraged to seek professional advice for specific issues related to their situation.

The opinions expressed in this book are those of the author and do not necessarily reflect the views of any affiliated organizations or institutions. The author and publisher disclaim any liability for any direct, indirect, incidental, or consequential damages arising from the use of the information contained in this book. All trademarks and other intellectual property rights are the property of their owners. Any product or service names used within this book may be trademarks or service marks of other persons or entities.

Preface

The journey to writing this book began 15 years ago when I first encountered the complex and fascinating world of natural gas trading. My experiences in the industry have been both challenging and rewarding, and it is my hope that this book will serve as a useful guide for others embarking on a similar path.

This book aims to demystify the basic concepts of natural gas trading, scheduling, and associated technologies that facilitate this process and provide practical insights that can be applied in real-world scenarios. It is intended for both beginners and seasoned professionals who wish to deepen their understanding of the field and increase their personal compensation.

I owe a debt of gratitude to my mentors, colleagues, and friends, whose unwavering support and profound wisdom have been the bedrock of my journey. Their insights and encouragement have been instrumental in shaping this book, making it a collaborative effort born from shared experiences and collective knowledge.

Writing this book has been a labor of love, fueled by a passion to share the insights and lessons that have shaped my career. I am thrilled to present it to you, with the hope that it will not only inform and educate but also inspire and challenge you to reach new heights in your own professional journey.

Thank you for reading.

Foreword
Fletcher Sturm

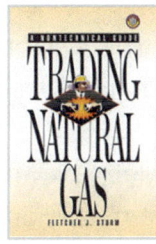

Author of *Trading Natural Gas: A Non-Technical Guide* (1996, 2020)

Welcome to a deep dive into the complex and ever-changing world of natural gas trading. As someone who has lived and breathed this industry for decades, and myself an author of a book about trading natural gas, I am excited to share insights that bridge both experience and innovation.

Natural gas trading is not merely about numbers and contracts; it's about problem-solving, teamwork, relationships, understanding the pulse of the market, recognizing the subtle shifts in trends, and leveraging technology to innovate. This book skillfully captures these nuances, providing a detailed exploration of trading strategies, scheduling logistics, and the technological advancements that are revolutionizing the industry.

Over the years, the natural gas market has witnessed monumental changes—from my early days before basis markets were a thing to the recent surge in AI and automation. This guide meticulously covers everything from the basics of the trading market to recent developments, blending practical advice with real-world scenarios that bring the subject matter to life in an engaging and often humorous way.

This book aims to demystify the fundamentals while also delving into the more intricate aspects of natural gas trading. Whether you're a novice scheduler or a seasoned trader, you'll find valuable knowledge and strategies that can enhance your understanding and performance in this market that has something for everyone.

As you turn these pages, you'll encounter wisdom from industry veterans, practical applications of economic principles, and strategic approaches to market participation. The insights shared here are designed to help you navigate the complexities of the market and achieve success.

On a personal note, I want to acknowledge my friend Jay Bhatty, the author of this book. Jay and I first met at an industry conference some years ago, and since then, we've stayed in touch, sharing ideas on technology, environmental commodities, and our shared passion for the natty gas. His dedication to this field and his wealth of knowledge are evident throughout this book.

I encourage you to immerse yourself in this comprehensive guide and use its wisdom to advance your career and deepen your understanding of natural gas trading.

Introduction

An Insider's Guide to Accumulating Wealth in the Nat Gas Industry

I was born in Mumbai, India, and lived there until the age of 17. I have the fondest memories of growing up there, and I still visit India at least once a year. During my childhood, chronic electricity shortages were common. That always intrigued me and is probably the reason that I remain fascinated with energy markets to this day. Both my grandfather and father were entrepreneurs. When I was 12 years old, my grandfather shared with me his life experiences about how he fought to gain India's freedom from the British in 1947 and how he was even jailed as a freedom fighter. He later introduced TVs to India, for which he received an award from Prime Minister Indira Gandhi for bringing TVs to the masses. He inculcated in me the desire to become an entrepreneur and take calculated risks.

I came to the U.S. as an undergraduate student and majored in economics. My senior year paper was a thesis on the deregulation of the energy industry. That paper piqued my interest in the U.S. energy markets, which prompted me to graduate from my college in Ohio and head to Houston, Texas, the energy capital of the world. I was a naive analyst when I joined Enron. I loved the company and learned a lot about natural gas trading. Although Enron failed, I still kept in touch with many alumni who later went on to become veterans in the industry.

I started scheduling natural gas at JPMorgan Bank in 2008. I remember my first day on the job like it was yesterday. Hurricane Ike was about to make landfall in Houston the day after I started work. There was chaos on the trade floor as everyone was trying to determine what impact the hurricane would have on gas flowing through various pipelines. No one knew which pipelines might curtail gas flow, thereby affecting the profits and losses of many gas traders throughout the country. I was still trying to log into my newly assigned computer with four monitors. As I was setting up my password for my new JPMorgan email account, someone tapped me on my shoulder and said, "Hi, Jay, I'm Paul Posoli, the head of the trade floor." I knew exactly who Paul was, but I was surprised he knew who I was. Paul was my boss's boss's boss! I was quite impressed by Paul's ability to connect with new employees and make them feel comfortable on their first day on the trade floor.

Just a few months prior to my start date, JPMorgan had acquired the failed investment bank Bear Stearns in March 2008. The entire Houston trade floor was comprised of ex-Bear Stearns traders. On March 16, 2008, Bear Stearns, the 85-year-old investment bank, narrowly avoided bankruptcy by its sale to JPMorgan Chase at the shockingly low price of $2 per share.

In early 2007, Bear Stearns seemed to be riding high with a stock market capitalization of $20 billion. But its increasing involvement in the hedge-fund business, particularly with risky mortgage-backed securities, paved the way for it to become one of the earliest casualties of the subprime mortgage crisis that led to the Great Recession of 2008. After the New York Stock Exchange opened on Friday, March 14, 2008, Bear's stock price began plummeting. The next day, JPMorgan Chase concluded that Bear Stearns was worth only $236 million. Desperately seeking a solution that would stop Bear's failure from spreading to other over-leveraged banks (such as Merrill Lynch, Lehman Brothers, and Citigroup), the Federal Reserve called its first emergency weekend meeting in 30 years. On Sunday evening, March 16, 2008, Bear's board of directors agreed to sell the firm to JPMorgan Chase for $2 per share—a 93 percent discount from Bear's closing stock price on Friday. The unexpected downfall of the nation's storied, fifth-largest investment bank, founded in 1923, shocked the financial world and sent global markets tumbling. As it turned out, Bear Stearns would be only the first in a string of financial firms brought down by a classic "run on the bank."

In September 2008, the same month that I started my job on the JPMorgan trade floor, Bank of America quickly purchased the struggling Merrill Lynch, while venerable Lehman Brothers collapsed into bankruptcy, a stunning failure that would kick off an international banking crisis and drive the nation into the biggest economic meltdown since the Great Depression. Not many people knew this, but Bear Stearns had a very profitable natural gas trading desk, which now fell into JPMorgan's lap. This was the backdrop of my first day on the job. Banks were laying off employees by the thousands every month. Working at a bank offered the least job security when I showed up to work. This stress was magnified by the fact that a hurricane was about to hit the next day, which would probably cause financial losses for JPMorgan's natural gas trading desk.

There was no book or manual that I could read in order to understand how to schedule gas on an interstate natural gas pipeline. I was tasked with scheduling gas across 15 pipelines, an unusually large number of pipes for a newbie. I would have to work on the weekend as well, as this was crunch time. Any pipeline could announce an operational flow order (OFO), which is an event of force majeure. This allows pipelines to curtail gas flows to any shipper due to hurricane activity or any other event outside of the pipeline's control.

I was copiously jotting down handwritten notes into my journal as I shadowed a senior scheduler, who was training me on how to input gas nominations into a pipeline electronic bulletin board (EBB). A gas nomination is an electronic order to inform the pipeline to flow gas from one location to another on a certain date. It involved triple entry of nominations. The first-time schedulers enter nominations into their spreadsheets. There may be multiple spreadsheets for each pipeline. Since I was scheduling gas across 15 pipelines, I was simultaneously updating around 25 spreadsheets every minute of the day across my four computer monitors.

The second-time schedulers replicate this process by entering the same nominations into every pipeline's EBB. Each spreadsheet must match each EBB. The third-time schedulers perform data duplication by entering the same "noms" yet again into JPMorgan's trade capture system. All three systems of record have to be in sync. If gas is cut, all three systems need to be updated. I was constantly chasing my tail each time gas got cut. At that time, I had an epiphany! *There's gotta be one portal instead of fifteen different EBBs!* The more pipelines a company traded across, the more cumbersome the process of gas scheduling became.

When we search for a hotel or an airline ticket, we go to one website, like Kayak or Expedia. Why can't we have the same in the natural gas world? That's when the idea of NatGasHub.com was born. I built this app to reduce the pain points that I faced on the job during my first few months. Today, NatGasHub.com has become the industry standard to submit automated gas noms to multiple pipelines without doing any hand-typing or manual data entry. I wish such a tool had been available on my first day on the job. I had studied at Cornell University, but I had never come across a single course in Cornell's entire course catalog that taught a student how to trade or schedule natural gas. This is one of my primary reasons for writing this book.

The role of a natural gas scheduler or trader is highly deadline-oriented, requires attention to detail, is stressful, and is mentally and physically challenging. The burden rests on the schedulers' shoulders to ensure that gas flows every day so that no one is left without energy. When we flip a switch and turn on the light, rarely do we think about everything that went on behind the scenes to make the lightbulb turn on. Natural gas schedulers and traders keep your lights on—literally!

In this book, I will discuss how profits can be made trading natural gas, using both physical and financial instruments. I will also reveal how you can land lucrative six-figure and higher-paying jobs in natural gas trading and scheduling. (Hint: It's a club!) For traders, I will divulge ten strategies that could make you $10 million per year in trading profits. These are pearls of wisdom revealed by successful natural gas traders whom I have interviewed in order to write this book. You will hear real strategies implemented by experienced natural gas traders, as a result of which they were able to increase their take-home pay from $150,000 per year to $4 million-plus per year. This is the book you've been waiting for to realize your dream of Nat Gas Million$.

For schedulers, I will disclose the tricks to understanding nomination models across over 100 different pipelines. Although each pipeline's website looks different to you, after reading this book, you will discover that all the 100-plus pipeline nomination interfaces can be standardized into four neat models. This will help you schedule gas more easily and provide a new level of confidence in mastering the art of natural gas scheduling. Starting schedulers making $60,000 to $70,000 per year will discover what it takes to double their take-home pay. In addition to pay hikes, you will learn how heads of trading make decisions about your annual bonuses. Once you know these levers, you will be able to maximize your total annual compensation and achieve your lifetime financial goals sooner.

For technologists, I will reveal different ways in which traders and technology professionals are employing artificial intelligence (AI) and robotic process automation (RPA) to turbocharge their company profits. Implementing some of these strategies will result in guaranteed demonstrable savings for your technology bosses. You will be able to check the AI checkbox on your annual goals list and establish yourself as the resident tech expert within your organization. You will also discover how digital labor can be used to enhance human labor. Robots don't get tired, don't go on lunch breaks, and don't ask for pay hikes. When you augment your company's human labor with digital labor, you will be able to demonstrate to your management the increased profits that result from lower labor costs. For each dollar in reduced labor costs, you will be able to convince your management to reward you financially with a higher paycheck while still enhancing the company's bottom line. You can tie your paycheck directly to the savings you help your company realize by implementing new technologies, specifically RPA and AI. Being a first mover by using RPA and AI to enhance natural gas profits will boost your career prospects as well as establish you as an authority within your industry.

However, before you read about these money-making concepts, you need to understand the fundamentals. As they say in sports, fundamentals are everything.

Natural Gas

The Most Important Commodity of Our Lives

"Energy can be neither created nor destroyed."

— **First Law of Thermodynamics**

In a small village, an old blacksmith named Tomas had a unique forge. One day, a curious boy named Eli asked, "How does the fire keep burning?"

Tomas smiled. "Energy is like a river, Eli. It flows and changes form but never disappears."

Eli watched as Tomas hammered a piece of iron, sparks flying. "This iron was once part of a mountain, shaped by the Earth's energy. The fire that heats it now comes from the wood, which grows because of the sun's energy," Tomas continued.

Eli's eyes widened with understanding. "So the energy just changes form?"

"Exactly," Tomas nodded. "Nothing is ever lost. The energy in the fire will forge this iron into something new, but the energy itself remains."

Years later, Eli became a blacksmith, passing on Tomas's wisdom. The village thrived, each generation understanding that energy is a constant force, always transforming but never vanishing.

When you flip a switch in your house, the electricity that illuminates your room likely came from one of these sources:

1. A solar panel (solar energy converted to electrical energy)
2. A windmill (kinetic energy converted to electrical energy)
3. A nuclear plant (nuclear energy converted to electrical energy)
4. A natural gas turbine (thermal energy converted to electrical energy)
5. A coal plant (chemical energy converted to electrical energy)
6. A hydro project, such as the Hoover Dam (gravitational potential energy converted to electrical energy)

In each of these cases, energy was neither created nor destroyed. It was simply converted from one form to another. In 2022, natural gas accounted for approximately 40 percent of the electricity generation in the United States. This makes it one of the primary sources of electricity generation in the country.[1]

To replace the approximate 20 percent share of coal (which has the highest carbon content), natural gas is one of the best options available today. This is because it has a lower carbon footprint than coal, is available in plentiful supply in the U.S., is cheap, is easily transportable over the pipeline infrastructure already built, and can provide reliable uninterrupted electricity 24 hours a day, 7 days a week.

Not only is natural gas used in electricity generation, but it is also a primary input feedstock for fertilizer production, which in turn facilitates food production. Because natural gas serves as a feedstock for both electricity and food, that makes natural gas the most valuable commodity of our lives.

---

1 "Electricity Explained: Electricity in the United States," EIA.gov, last updated June 30, 2023, https://www.eia.gov/energyexplained/electricity/electricity-in-the-us.php.

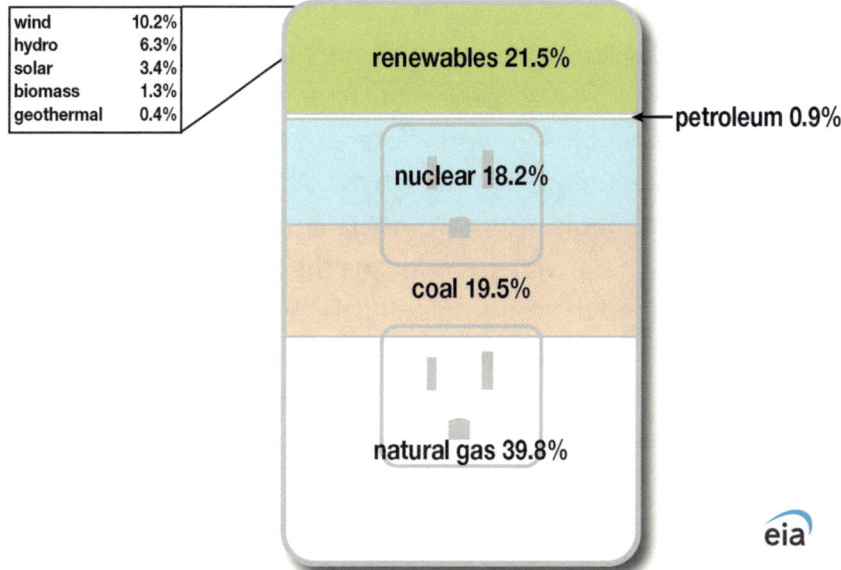

Data source: U.S. Energy Information Administration, *Electric Power Monthly*, February 2023, preliminary data
Note: Includes generation from power plants with at least 1,000 kilowatts of electric generation capacity (utility-scale). Hydro is conventional hydroelectric. Petroleum includes petroleum liquids, petroleum coke, other gases, hydroelectric pumped storage, and other sources.

When I first stepped foot on the JPMorgan trade floor, I had the impression of a vast arena filled with multiple monitors displaying a whirlwind of data. The air is electric, charged with the urgency of decisions made in split seconds. Traders shout buy and sell orders, their voices blending into a symphony of ambition and strategy. Amid this fast-paced frenzy, camaraderie flourishes, with colleagues sharing information rapidly and seamlessly. Sharp instincts and quick calculations guide every move, as millions of dollars change hands every minute of the day. The aroma of fresh coffee heightens the senses. Heroes will be forged in the crucible of the market each day. The adrenaline courses through your veins, intoxicating and exhilarating, with rewards beyond imagination. How could you not be fascinated by the thrill of trading?

Here, every second counts, and the glamour of the financial world is palpable, driven by teamwork and a relentless pursuit of success. The trade floor is a theater of high stakes and high rewards, where the thrill of the market's pulse fuels the relentless drive for victory.

After one year on the job as a gas scheduler, I was promoted to a gas trader. As I stepped onto the trade floor that day, my eyes were wide with anticipation. Monitors flickered with data, and the buzz of activity was electrifying. I felt a rush as I placed my first trade. But within moments, panic set in—I'd made a multimillion-dollar mistake by clicking on the wrong product on the ICE trading screen. My heart pounded and the room spinning. How could I be so careless in doing something I had waited my whole career for? Maybe it was the adrenaline that made me jittery. Just then, a seasoned trader named Tom stepped in. With swift precision, Tom corrected the blunder, leveraging his vast experience to turn the tide. I watched in relief as the catastrophe was averted. "Remember, kid," Tom said with a grin, "we're a team here." That's when I realized the adrenaline, the stakes, the camaraderie—it was all real!

Introduction for Nat Gas Traders

"Fundamentals are the foundation for success. We can't skip the basics and expect to be great."

— Michael Jordan, Chicago Bulls, NBA Champion

Ryan, a fresh graduate from Lubbock, Texas, stumbled upon natural gas trading with zero industry knowledge. Armed only with a determination to succeed, he devoured every resource on trading fundamentals. Late nights and relentless practice honed his skills. One pivotal trade, based on a brilliant strategy he devised, skyrocketed his earnings. Within a year, Ryan transformed from a novice to a millionaire trader, his name whispered in awe across trading floors. His journey from clueless beginner to industry titan proves that mastery of basics can indeed lead to unimaginable wealth. The key to being successful in the nat gas industry is understanding the basics, the nuts and bolts, of how natural gas is bought, sold, and flowed through the North American pipeline system. To understand this, let's take a look at the instruments available to a trader to manage buys and sells.

Types of Instruments Traded

Physical natural gas instruments:

1. Storage
2. Transport
3. Parks or Loans
4. Physical Options

Financial natural gas instruments:

1. Natural gas futures
2. Natural gas swaps
3. Financial options

Physical natural gas: In order to buy natural gas, a buyer must determine whether they want to pay a fixed price or a floating price. This decision is driven by how much risk a trader wants to take. A fixed price transaction has a much higher risk than a floating price. Why is this? Let's take an example. Let's assume I work for a natural gas utility in Chicago. I need to buy physical natural gas so that homes and businesses in Chicago can stay warm in the winter by burning natural gas. I contact a gas producer in Houston, who offers me two options. One of them is to buy gas at a fixed price of $5 per MMBtu for delivery in the winter months. The other option is to buy gas at a floating price at Henry Hub (HH) futures plus a $0.50 per MMBtu premium.

> Let's assume today is July 1:
>
> Fixed Price Offered = $5 per MMBtu for delivery from December 1 to December 31
>
> Floating Price Offered = HH futures + $0.50 for delivery from December 1 to December 31

If I buy gas at a fixed price of $5 today, and the fixed price of gas on December 1 drops to $2.50/MMBtu (due to supply-and-demand issues), I overpaid by 100 percent, versus if I had just waited and not bought the gas in advance. Contrast this with the floating price scenario. Between July 1 and December 1, I am not exposed to the price fluctuation, as I will pay whatever the floating price settles at. As a gas utility, I want to minimize my risk (which in this case is exposure to price fluctuations) so that I stay in business. Hence, I will choose a floating price. In the natural gas markets, this floating price is also referred to as an "index" price: for example, Chicago Citygate Index. The fixed price trade has a higher volatility versus the floating price trade. Different traders in the market are willing to take different risks. This is what creates trading opportunities in the natural gas market, or for that matter, any market.

I like to view energy traders as glorified insurance agents. Think about why you buy different kinds of insurance. For example, you buy car insurance to protect yourself from the unpredictable cost of wrecking someone's Porsche. You buy medical insurance to protect yourself from the unpredictable cost of having to pay for a costly cancer treatment. You buy home insurance to protect yourself from the unpredictable cost of rebuilding your home should it be wiped out by a hurricane. Similarly, the Chicago gas buyer needs to be protected from the price of gas running up in the winter and wiping out mom-and-pop retail stores that can't afford expensive heating bills. We all need insurance agents to protect us from risks in life. Risk can never just vanish into thin air. It can only be mitigated through risk transfer to someone else.

Why would someone else want to take on your risk? The simple answer is "for money." This is why insurance companies exist. If they didn't, we wouldn't be able to carry on with our daily lives. Many of us would be wiped out trying to live our lives unprotected against the forces at work every day in the real world. But insurance is a risky business. You need deep pockets to underwrite insurance. In the words of Warren Buffet (who owns one of the largest insurance companies in the world), "In the insurance business, there is no statute of limitation on stupidity. We regularly pay for mistakes made 20 years ago, and we will keep doing so." This is what energy traders do. They take away the risk someone else does not want to take in the hopes of making money (a trading profit).

One of the biggest face-offs in the natural gas markets happened between John Arnold (the legendary natural gas trader who worked at Enron and then at his own hedge fund, Centaurus) and Brian Hunter, who worked at the hedge fund Amaranth. If they made a Hollywood movie about traders in the natural gas industry, this incident would be the cliffhanger moment. In September 2006, both John Arnold and Brian Hunter were on opposite sides of the same trade. A $6 billion trade! It was a high-stakes, winner-take-all gamble.

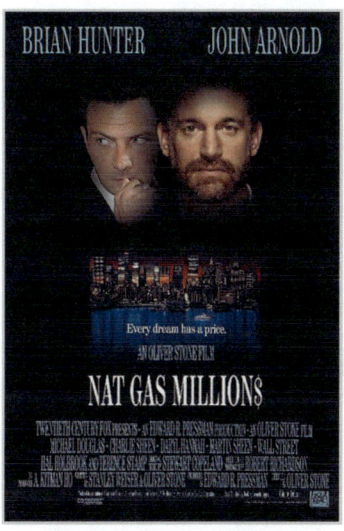

Hunter made bullish bets on natural gas by buying natural gas futures contracts in one month and selling them in another, thereby creating an intermonth March–April spread. In September 2006, he established this trading position by buying and selling the 2007 March–April spread. Hunter made risky decisions on natural gas, hoping the tropical storms would shut down production. That happened the previous year (in 2005) because of Hurricane Katrina, which led to a spike in the natural gas price. However, history didn't repeat itself in 2006. Storms in the summer of 2006 didn't have a significant impact on natural gas production, and the March–April price spread moved against Hunter.

When the markets opened for trading the next day, John Arnold experienced a windfall profit of over $6 billion, which cemented his position on the Forbes list of the most wealthy people in the world. Meanwhile, Brian Hunter was lost in oblivion after his hedge fund was forced to liquidate in bankruptcy. Hunter's positions were so enormous he wasn't able to liquidate them, resulting in fatal losses. This loss was the biggest since the collapse of Long-Term Capital Management in 1998. This is also why trading large positions in the natural gas market are now referred to as "widow-maker" trades, particularly due to the extreme volatility and concentrated risks amassed, often intentionally, by many traders, in the hopes of making windfall profits. This is probably why energy traders are sometimes referred to as cowboys.

Don't end up like Hunter!

Three Equations Every Trader Must Know

Now we understand why some traders want exposure to floating price risk, versus others who want exposure to fixed price risk. Some traders take on both types of risks, intentionally, unintentionally (like when a trader doesn't understand how the market works), or because they have no other option (for example, due to limited supply or demand of gas at a particular location). The equations shown below help a trader disaggregate the risk into components and insulate him or her from chunks of risk. Here are the three cardinal equations every natural gas trader must know to be successful (like John Arnold):

Memorize these!

1. Fixed price physical (FPP) = futures (F) + financial basis (FB) + physical index (PI)
2. Fixed price financial (FPF) = futures (F) + financial basis (FB)
3. Physical basis (PB) = financial basis (FB) + physical index (PI)

They are as true as 3 + 2 = 5. These are mathematical truisms and will help you make a lot of money or shed unwanted risk quickly and with surgical precision. They are what you need to make it to the Nat Gas Hall of Fame!

Let's dissect these three equations to understand why they are true. Once you understand why they are true, then all you need to do is memorize them and use them in trading or risk management every day. Before we start, we need to go over some definitions. I've defined each of the variables in these three equations below.

The best analogy to understand how the natural gas industry works is to use the airline industry. Here are how the industries are similar:

Pipeline Industry Comparison to Travel Industry

AIRLINE TICKET	PIPELINE CONTRACT
1. Ticket Number	1. Service Requestor Contract #
2. Passenger Name	2. Shipper Name
3. Passenger Passport #	3. Shipper DUNS #
4. Travel Class	4. Rate Schedule
5. Confirmation Status	5. Firm/Interruptible
6. Departure City	6. Receipt Location
7. Destination City	7. Delivery Location
8. Departure Date	8. Flow Start Date
9. Arrival Date	9. Flow End Date
10. Bags	10. Natural Gas Volume
11. Pay Airline Fare	11. Pay Pipeline Tariff

Fixed price physical (FPP): This involves buying physical (not financial) natural gas at a fixed price per MMBtu (for example, $5.73/MMBtu) for delivery to a specific location on a pipeline for a specific flow date (for example, March 23) for a specific flow period (for example, one day or one month). The word physical implies that actual natural gas molecules will be delivered by the seller to the buyer on a natural gas pipeline. The parties may agree mutually to allow delivery on either a firm or interruptible basis. Firm delivery is like traveling with a confirmed seat on an airplane. Interruptible delivery is like traveling standby on an airplane.

Futures (F): This is the ICE® Henry LD1 Fixed Price Futures contract. It is a monthly cash settled exchange futures contract based upon the monthly price published by New York Mercantile Exchange (NYMEX). "Henry" stands for the physical pipeline location called Henry Hub in Erath, Louisiana, where several different natural gas pipelines intersect. "L1D" stands for "last one day." It is the last scheduled trading day of the NYMEX Henry Hub natural gas futures contract for a particular delivery date. Because this is a cash settled contract, it is referred to as a "financial" as opposed to a "physical" contract.

It is important to note here that a financial futures contract *could* be purchased in order to buy physical molecules of natural gas. However, in practice, this rarely happens. If someone wants physical natural gas molecules, they will buy fixed price physical gas, which is a separate instrument we defined above. The reason traders are trading the financial contract is specifically because they do not want to make or take delivery of physical gas. Think of a fixed price physical contract as a real, physical dollar bill that you can hold in your hand. By contrast, a financial dollar bill is something that is in your bank account and can be converted to a physical dollar bill if you go to the bank and physically withdraw it. It has the same underlying value, that is, one dollar.

Most Henry Hub natural gas futures contracts do not result in physical delivery of natural gas. Instead, they are typically settled financially by offsetting the obligations to buy and sell, with very few transactions involving an actual exchange of the physical commodity. This is common in most futures (oil, electricity, metals) markets, where the futures contracts serve more as financial tools for hedging and price speculation rather than for procuring physical goods.

Physical basis (PB): *Basis* is defined as the difference in price of natural gas at the Henry Hub location versus at any other location in North America. The basis could be a positive difference (premium) or a negative differential (discount) to the Henry Hub price. It represents the additional premium or discount it costs for someone to deliver gas to any location in North America, using the Henry Hub as a reference point. The fundamental assumption here is that natural gas is a fungible commodity and has the same characteristics in every corner of North America. This is true in the natural gas market because fortunately, the entire pipeline system in North America forces producers to standardize their natural gas, that is, to make it of the same quality (when it comes to contents like water vapor, methane, and so on), no matter where the gas was drilled. This is not true in the crude oil market, where there are several grades, such as light crude, sour crude, and so on.

Let's understand basis with some examples. If the price of physical natural gas at Henry Hub is, say, $5.00/MMBtu, and the price for delivering gas to New York is $6.00, then the New York basis price is +$1.00. Similarly, if the price for delivering natural gas to Los Angeles is $4.00, then the Los Angeles basis price is –$1.00. It can be confusing to many people to think about negative prices. This was one of the things I found confusing as well when I started my career as a natural gas trader. Unfortunately, there was no book that explained this concept well. The only way to learn was by asking other natural gas traders. But here is a simple trick to understanding natural gas basis. Think of basis as an object (such as a car or a chair) that has some financial value. You may have studied the concept of a number line (shown below) in high school math. Zero is in the middle of the number line. Values to the left go from zero all the way to negative infinity. Values to the right go all the way from zero to positive infinity. A basis price could assume any of these values between negative infinity and positive infinity. For rural areas (such as Fargo, North Dakota), it is cheaper to deliver goods relative to Henry Hub (nothing against North Dakota; I love rural areas!). Thus, North Dakota would be to the left of zero because it has a negative basis price. For congested, populated areas (such as New York or Chicago), it is more expensive to deliver goods relative to Henry Hub. Thus, these congested areas have a positive basis price.

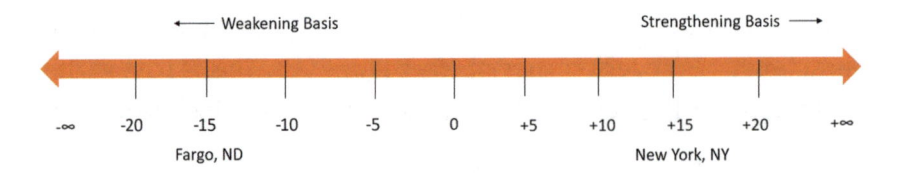

⟵ Weakening Basis   Strengthening Basis ⟶

-∞   -20   -15   -10   -5   0   +5   +10   +15   +20   +∞
            Fargo, ND   New York, NY

When a trader makes a statement that "basis is strengthening," it means that the price is moving to the right. When a trader says, "basis is weakening," it means the price is moving to the left.

Financial basis (FB): To understand financial basis, let's first start with physical basis, which we defined above. The word *physical* implies that actual natural gas molecules will be delivered by the seller to the buyer on a natural gas pipeline. Here is a trick to think about any financial product in the nat gas market. If you take the physical molecules away from the physical product, you're left with just a financial product. You can see this in the diagram below. Item 1 is the physical molecules that make up the physical basis product (Item 3). Item 2 is the financial basis product. Hence, Item 1 + Item 2 = Item 3.

Physical Basis
ITEM 1

Item 1 = Item 2 + Item 3

Physical Index (Gas Molecules)
ITEM 2

Financial Basis (Paper Only)
ITEM 3

Physical index (PI): This product consists of physical molecules priced at a monthly index price (for example, Inside Federal Energy Regulatory Commission [IFERC] Chicago Citygate) or at a daily index price (for example, Gas Daily [GD] Chicago Citygate).

Now let's put all three equations together. Using T-charts, we will see why and how these three equations are categorically mathematically true.

Equation 1: FPP = F + FB + PI
Equation 2: FPF = F + FB
Equation 3: PB = FB + PI

T-charts are great because you can put all your "buys" on one side and all your "sells" on the other side. You can see how the common elements cancel each other out. What is left is your profit or loss. It also keeps you real because it gives you an accountant's view of your risk profile. We all know how diligently accountants work. Every credit or debit must be recorded and balanced out. There can be no "funny money."

A few words about T-charts:

We will put "buys" on the left and "sells" on the right side of the T-charts.

Important Concept: Physical Versus Financial

When you display a physical transaction on a T-chart, it is a one-sided transaction. By one-sided, I mean it will either be displayed on the left-hand side of the T-chart or the right-hand side, but not both. This is because a physical transaction involves the movement of physical natural gas molecules from the seller to the buyer of gas. At any given point in time, the molecules are held by either the buyer or the seller, but not both. Hence, it is displayed only on one side of the T-chart. Title transfer of these molecules happens at the time of trade consummation.

When you display a financial transaction on a T-chart, it is a two-sided transaction. This means it is displayed on *both* sides of the T-chart. This is because it is a financial transaction in which one party (buyer or seller) swaps one cashflow for another with the other party. There are no physical molecules exchanged in a financial transaction. Only cashflows are exchanged.

A financial transaction exists for the purpose of risk management of the physical transaction. When you combine both physical and financial transactions, a trader has more flexibility to manage risk.

> *"The essence of investment management is the management of risks, not the management of returns."*
>
> — **BENJAMIN GRAHAM**, Father of Value Investing

A trader can do a physical transaction with one company (for example, a small gas producer), and then do a financial transaction with a different company (for example, a hedge fund). This increases liquidity (number of traders) in the market because the gas producer may not want to do a financial transaction. Conversely, a hedge fund may not want to do a physical transaction. By having many companies participate in the market, a trader has many options. This also leads to price transparency. These are the features of any efficient market: high liquidity, price transparency, and market depth (meaning that there are buy and sell orders at various prices, which provides a buffer against large price swings. This depth ensures that large orders do not disproportionately impact the market price).

For buys on the T-chart, the prices numbers are negative. For sells, they are positive.

For all examples in the T-chart, the volumes for each trade are assumed to be the same.

Let's Look at Equation 1 of 3

This says that buying FPP gas is the same as selling an F contract plus an FB contract plus a PI. For simplicity, let's assume the volume for each transaction is the same, for example, 10,000 MMBtus.

Equation 1:

FIXED PRICE PHYSICAL (FPP) = FUTURES (F) + FINANCIAL BASIS (FB) + PHYSICAL INDEX (PI)

Trade 1: The FPP trade is represented in the T-chart on the buy side. Since this is a physical transaction, it is one-sided. Thus, there is nothing on the sell side. In this example, I've bought El Paso fixed price physical gas at $5.50 per MMBtu.

Trade 2: The F trade involves selling a futures contract. I have shown $5.00 on the sell side of the T-chart. This is a financial transaction and hence has two sides. On the buy side of the T-chart, I have shown L1D. This is the symbol for the futures settlement price, which the trader will receive upon the contract being settled. It is the last price traded on the last day of the life of this futures contract. Technically, it is the weighted average of the prices traded in the last 30 minutes of the life of this contract.

Trade 3: The FB trade is also a financial trade and hence will be displayed on both sides of the T-chart. A financial basis swap by definition involves swapping the L1D cashflow for the El Paso IFERC cashflow. When I sell financial basis, I'm paying the L1D cashflow and receiving the IFERC cashflow. Conversely, when I buy financial basis, I'm receiving the L1D cashflow and paying the IFERC cashflow. If this is confusing, here's a simple rule. If you're a basis seller, the L1D goes on the sell side. If you're a basis buyer, the L1D goes on the buy side. Once you know which side to place the L1D cashflow on, the IFERC cashflow automatically goes to the opposite side. In this example, the location of the basis trade is El Paso. But it could be any location. The math stays the same.

Trade 4: The PI (as the name suggests) is a physical trade and hence is one-sided. I've placed the IFERC price on the sell side of the T-chart.

	1 Buy Trade, 3 Sell Trades		
	BUY	SELL	
1. FIXED PRICE PHYSICAL (FPP)	($5.50)		
	L1D $5.00		2. FUTURES (F)
	El Paso IFERC L1D + $0.50		3. FINANCIAL BASIS (FB)
		El Paso IFERC + $0.02	4. PHYSICAL INDEX (PI)
	($5.50)	$5.52	
		$0.02	Profit/Loss

Now that I have all four trades placed on the T-chart, let's cancel out any "legs" that negate each other. The L1D buy of the futures (F) trade negates the L1D sell of the financial basis (FB) trade. Thus, both these legs are cancelled out. Another way to think about this is that if I'm buying and selling the same thing, my risk is zero. Similarly, the El Paso IFERC leg on the buy side of the financial basis (FB) trade cancels out the El Paso IFERC leg of the physical index (PI) trade. After cancelling out these four legs, we're left with a profit of $0.02. We made an assumption earlier that the volume of each trade was 10,000 MMBtus. Let's say the duration was one month. Hence, the dollar profit on this trade is $0.02 per MMBtu × 10,000 MMBtus × 31 days = +$6,200. Not a bad day!

Key Takeaway

Whenever I buy something, I must sell something to stay hedged. Not hedging is a form of speculation. Think of each of the four variables in equation 1 (FPP, F, FB, and PI) as things. In this example, I bought one thing: FPP. To hedge it, I sold three things: F + FB + PI. But what would happen if I did not sell PI? Then I would be unhedged or not properly hedged.

Consider this. What would happen if instead of El Paso PI, I sold San Juan PI for the same volume? Would I be hedged? No, because I'm not hedging apples with apples. In trader lingo, this is referred to as a "dirty hedge." This is because the El Paso location is different from the San Juan location. By trading one for the other, I've introduced a new type of risk into my portfolio. Traders may sometimes do this if there is not enough liquidity in one region relative to another. Many traders are forced to carry dirty hedges in their portfolios. As the legendary trader Jim Simons of Renaissance Technologies once said, "The only perfect hedge is a Japanese garden."

Consider another scenario. I bought FPP. Which of these things—F, FB, or PI—has the most risk, and which one has the least? The F or futures contract has the most risk. This is because a futures contract has an outright price, which could run up from zero to infinity. If I need to buy a futures contract and the market starts running away from me, theoretically the price could run up to any number. Hence, this is the riskiest part of my trade. I would want to hedge this first. The next riskiest thing is the financial basis swap. The reason this is not as risky as the futures contract is because the financial basis swap is the difference between the futures price versus the IFERC price.

Recall that one side of the basis swap is represented as L1D (this is the futures price). The other side of the basis swap is represented by IFERC (index price). When I buy a basis swap, I'm long L1D and short IFERC. Vice versa, if I sell a basis swap. The least risky instrument is the PI (physical IFERC or GDD Index). This typically trades as a premium or discount. For example, the El Paso IFERC Index can be purchased at IFERC + $.01 or IFERC + $0.025 or IFERC + $0.04, and so on. Thus, my risk is the premium or the discount only, which is just a few pennies. Contrast the risk with the futures contract, which is an absolute price and could run up to infinity. Let's say the IFERC price settles at $5.00 for the month. Then I would pay this $5.00 price, plus or minus the premium or the discount. No matter what the IFERC settles at, my only risk is the premium or discount, which is a few pennies. Most of my risk has been hedged with the F (futures) contract. This barrel chart should help make things clear.

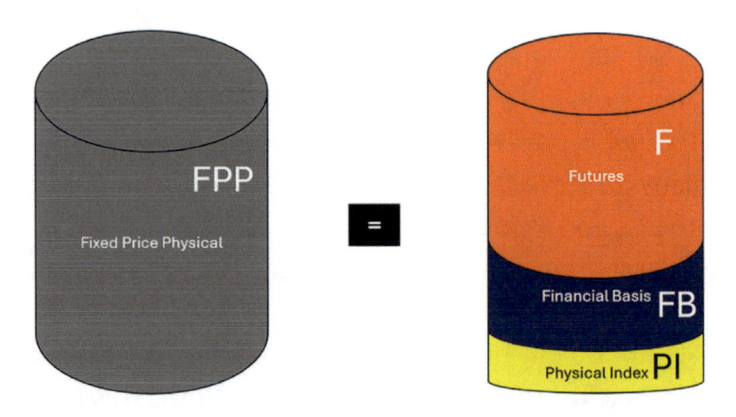

Consider yet another scenario: A trader bought FPP. Let's say they only sold FB and PI against it. They intentionally chose not to sell F. According to equation 1, in this case, the trader is "long" futures because they have too much of it. This means that if the futures price drops, it would hurt this trader. The reason they may choose to stay long (exposed) is that they have a bullish view of the futures price. They may choose to not hedge this piece of their risk. Not hedging is also considered speculation. Sometimes, a trader may unintentionally become unhedged (or exposed). This is because they may be executing hundreds of trades per day. They may think they have bought and sold all the things they need to stay hedged. But inadvertently, they may have missed something. This is why a trader needs to monitor their position in real time.

They must also review their position at the end of each trading session. When they come into the office the next morning, they must ensure their position is what they expect it to be. Some traders can sleep with a large amount of open (unhedged) risk in their book. Other traders prefer to be "flat," that is, having zero overnight risk. How much overnight risk a trader carries is a matter of personal preference. They must also ensure they stay within their approved risk tolerance measure. In most cases, this risk tolerance measure is referred to as value-at-risk (VaR). The concept of VaR would require an entire book to do justice. Hence, we will not get into the topic of VaR in this book.

A typical trader's position report looks like this, where the risk of each position is quantified with the riskiest position on top:

	Balance-of-Month	January	February	March	April	May	June	July	August	September	October	November	December
Fixed Price Physical (FPP)													
Chicago Citygate	5,000	10,000	10,000	10,000	10,000	10,000	10,000	10,000	10,000	10,000	10,000	10,000	10,000
Houston Ship Channel	7,000	25,000	25,000	25,000	25,000	25,000	25,000	25,000	25,000	25,000	25,000	25,000	25,000
Transco Zone 6 NY	9,000	15,000	15,000	15,000	15,000	15,000	15,000	15,000	15,000	15,000	15,000	15,000	15,000
Futures (F)													
L1D		500,000	500,000	500,000	500,000	500,000	500,000	500,000	500,000	500,000	500,000	500,000	500,000
Physical Basis (PB)													
Waha		12,000	12,000	12,000	12,000	12,000	12,000	12,000	12,000	12,000	12,000	12,000	12,000
Permian		200,000	200,000	200,000	200,000	200,000	200,000	200,000	200,000	200,000	200,000	200,000	200,000
San Juan		55,000	55,000	55,000	55,000	55,000	55,000	55,000	55,000	55,000	55,000	55,000	55,000
Socal		70,000	70,000	70,000	70,000	70,000	70,000	70,000	70,000	70,000	70,000	70,000	70,000
Financial Basis (FB)													
NGPL Texoke		30,000	30,000	30,000	30,000	30,000	30,000	30,000	30,000	30,000	30,000	30,000	30,000
NGPL Midcon		22,000	22,000	22,000	22,000	22,000	22,000	22,000	22,000	22,000	22,000	22,000	22,000
Monthly: IFERC Physical Index (PI)													
Algonquin	12,891	32,000	32,000	32,000	32,000	32,000	32,000	32,000	32,000	32,000	32,000	32,000	32,000
Panhandle	6,514	46,000	46,000	46,000	46,000	46,000	46,000	46,000	46,000	46,000	46,000	46,000	46,000
Trunkline	8,817	59,000	59,000	59,000	59,000	59,000	59,000	59,000	59,000	59,000	59,000	59,000	59,000
Daily: GDD Physical Index (PI)													
Florida Gas Zn 1	56,171	117,000	117,000	117,000	117,000	117,000	117,000	117,000	117,000	117,000	117,000	117,000	117,000

All volumes in MMBtus

The hierarchy of riskiest trades to least risky is shown below, with the riskiest instrument on top:

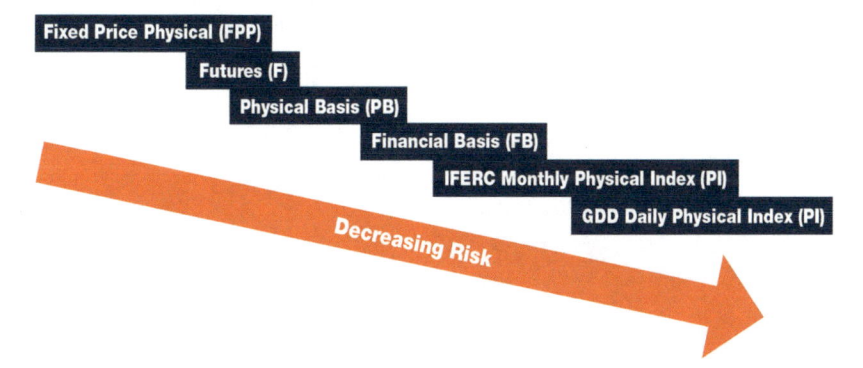

- Fixed Price Physical (FPP)
- Futures (F)
- Physical Basis (PB)
- Financial Basis (FB)
- IFERC Monthly Physical Index (PI)
- GDD Daily Physical Index (PI)

Decreasing Risk

The concept of risk management is important not just for traders but for companies too. For example, the biggest cost for an airline is the price of jet fuel. Many airlines do not hedge this price because they feel they are not traders and hence choose not to lock in this price. They prefer to be price-takers. But as I said earlier, not hedging is also a form of speculation. Not buying jet fuel is the same as putting your head in the sand and hoping the price of jet fuel doesn't run up. Hope is not a good strategy when it comes to risk management. My grandfather always said, "Hope for the best, but plan for the worst." This planning is what a trader would call prudent risk management. Every company should manage their risk prudently, whether their raw material is jet fuel, cocoa, coffee, natural gas, iron ore, computer chips, or any other commodity on this planet. As Mark Zuckerberg of Meta said, "The real risk is doing nothing."

> In the example, I've used a monthly index. Even if I use a daily index (for example, *Gas Daily* Daily Index), the math stays the same. I've shown a modified example below when a daily (versus) monthly index is involved. In this modified example, I would do a fifth trade, which is an IFERC versus *Gas Daily* daily swap. This is a financial trade and hence is displayed on both sides of the T-chart. In this swap, I'm swapping the El Paso IFERC Monthly Index for the El Paso *Gas Daily* Daily Index. The assumption made is this month has 30 days.

Three Equations Every Trader Must Know | 33

	1 Buy Trade, 4 Sell Trades		
	BUY	SELL	
1. FIXED PRICE PHYSICAL (FPP)	($5.50)		
	L1D $5.00		2. FUTURES (F)
	El Paso IFERC L1D + $0.50		3. FINANCIAL BASIS (FB)
	El Paso GDD (Days 1 to 30)	El Paso IFERC	5. IFERC Vs GAS DAILY SWAP
		Day 1 El Paso GDD + $0.02	4. PHYSICAL INDEX (PI)
		Day 2 El Paso GDD - $0.02	
		Day 3 El Paso GDD + $0.00	
		Day 4 El Paso GDD + $0.00	
		Day 5 El Paso GDD + $0.01	
		Day 6 El Paso GDD + $0.02	
		Day 7 El Paso GDD + $0.02	
		Day 8 El Paso GDD - $0.01	
		Day 9 El Paso GDD + $0.01	
		Day 10 El Paso GDD + $0.00	
		Days 11 to 30 El Paso GDD + $0.00	
	($5.50)	$5.55	
		$0.05	Profit/Loss

GDD = "Gas Daily" Publication's Daily Index

Let's Look at Equation 2 of 3

This says that buying fixed price financial (FPF) gas is the same as selling a futures (F) contract plus a financial basis (FB) contract. For simplicity, let's assume the volume for each transaction is the same: 10,000 MMBtus.

Equation 2: FIXED PRICE FINANCIAL (FPF) = FUTURES (F) / FINANCIAL BASIS (FB)

Trade 1: The fixed price financial trade is represented in the T-chart on the buy side. Since this is a financial transaction, it is two-sided. In this example, I've bought El Paso financial fixed price gas at $4.75 per MMBtu. On the sell side of the T-chart, I have displayed the El Paso IFERC Index.

Trade 2: The futures (F) trade involves selling a futures contract. I have shown $4.60 on the sell side of the T-chart. This is a financial transaction and hence has two sides. On the buy side of the T-chart, I have shown L1D. This is the symbol for the futures settlement price, which the trader will receive upon the contract being settled. It is the last price traded on the last day of the life of this futures contract. Technically, it is the weighted average of the prices traded in the last 30 minutes of the life of this contract.

Trade 3: The financial basis trade is also a financial trade and hence will be displayed on both sides of the T-chart. A financial basis swap by definition involves swapping the L1D cashflow for the El Paso IFERC cashflow. When I sell financial basis, I'm paying the L1D cashflow and receiving the IFERC cashflow. Conversely, when I buy financial basis, I'm receiving the L1D cashflow and paying the IFERC cashflow. If this is confusing, here's a simple rule. If you're a basis seller, the L1D goes on the sell side. If you're a basis buyer, the L1D goes on the buy side. Once you know which side to place the L1D cashflow on, the IFERC cashflow automatically goes to the opposite side. In this example, the location of the basis trade is El Paso. But it could be any location. The math stays the same.

	1 Buy Trade, 2 Sell Trades		
	BUY	SELL	
1. FIXED PRICE FINANCIAL (FPF)	($4.75)	El Paso IFERC	
	L1D	$4.60	2. FUTURES (F)
	El Paso IFERC	L1D + $0.50	3. FINANCIAL BASIS (FB)
	($4.75)	$5.10	
		$0.35	Profit/Loss

Now that I have all three trades placed on the T-chart, let's cancel out any legs that negate one another. The L1D buy of the futures (F) trade negates the L1D sell of the financial basis (FB) trade. Thus, both these legs are cancelled out. Another way to think about this is that if I'm buying and selling the same thing, my risk is zero. Similarly, the El Paso IFERC leg on the buy side of the financial basis (FB) trade cancels out the El Paso IFERC leg of the fixed price financial (FPF) trade. After cancelling out these four legs, we're left with a profit of $0.35 per MMBtu. We made an assumption earlier that the volume of each trade was 10,000 MMBtus. Let's say the duration was one month. Hence, the dollar profit on this trade is $0.35 per MMBtu × 10,000 MMBtus × 31 days = +$108,500. Cha-ching!

This bar chart displays the components of the fixed price financial (FPF) trade:

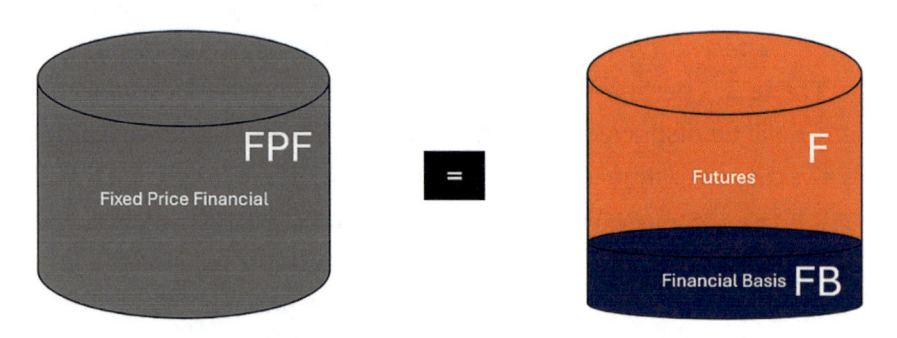

FPF
Fixed Price Financial
=
F
Futures
Financial Basis FB

Let's Look at Equation 3 of 3

This says that buying physical basis (PB) gas is the same as selling a financial basis (FB) contract plus a physical index (PI) contract. For simplicity, let's assume the volume for each transaction is the same: 10,000 MMBtus.

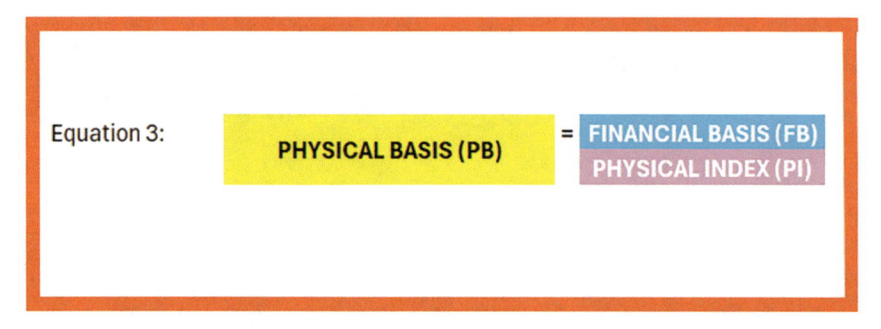

Equation 3: PHYSICAL BASIS (PB) = FINANCIAL BASIS (FB) PHYSICAL INDEX (PI)

Trade 1: The physical basis (PB) trade is represented in the T-chart on the buy side. Since this is a physical transaction, it is one-sided. In this example, I've bought El Paso physical basis gas at a price of L1D = $0.15 per MMBtu. L1D is the futures price for that month. The sell side is blank because this is a physical transaction.

Trade 2: The financial basis (FB) trade is a financial trade and hence will be displayed on both sides of the T-chart. A financial basis swap by definition involves swapping the L1D cashflow for the El Paso IFERC cashflow. When I sell financial basis, I'm paying the L1D cashflow and receiving the IFERC cashflow. Conversely, when I buy financial basis, I'm receiving the L1D cashflow and paying the IFERC cashflow. If this is confusing, here's a simple rule. If you're a basis seller, the L1D goes on the sell side. If you're a basis buyer, the L1D goes on the buy side. Once you know which side to place the L1D cashflow on, the IFERC cashflow automatically goes to the opposite side. In this example, the location of the basis trade is El Paso. But it could be any location. The math stays the same.

Trade 3: The physical index (as the name suggests) is a physical trade and hence is one-sided. I've placed the IFERC price on the sell side of the T-chart.

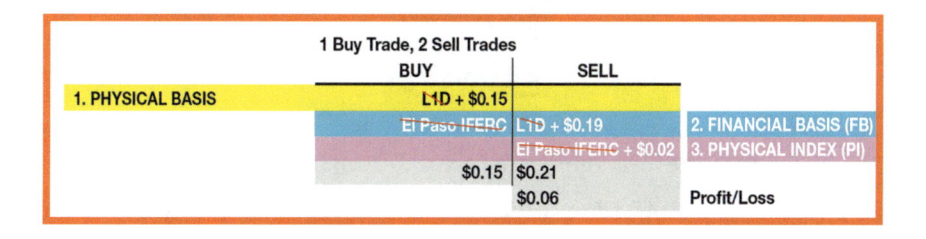

	1 Buy Trade, 2 Sell Trades		
	BUY	SELL	
1. PHYSICAL BASIS	L1D + $0.15		
	~~El Paso IFERC~~	~~L1D~~ + $0.19	2. FINANCIAL BASIS (FB)
		~~El Paso IFERC~~ + $0.02	3. PHYSICAL INDEX (PI)
	$0.15	$0.21	
		$0.06	Profit/Loss

Now that I have all three trades placed on the T-chart, let's cancel out any legs that negate one another. The L1D buy of the physical basis (PB) trade negates the L1D sell of the financial basis (FB) trade. Thus, both these legs are cancelled out. Another way to think about this is that if I'm buying and selling the same thing, my risk is zero. Similarly, the El Paso IFERC leg on the buy side of the financial basis (FB) trade cancels out the El Paso IFERC leg of the physical index (PI) trade. After cancelling out these four legs, we're left with a profit of $0.06. We made an assumption earlier that the volume of each trade was 10,000 MMBtus. Let's say the duration was one month. Hence, the dollar profit on this trade is $0.06 per MMBtu × 10,000 MMBtus × 31 days = +$18,600. Suh-weet!

This bar chart displays the components of the physical basis (PB) trade:

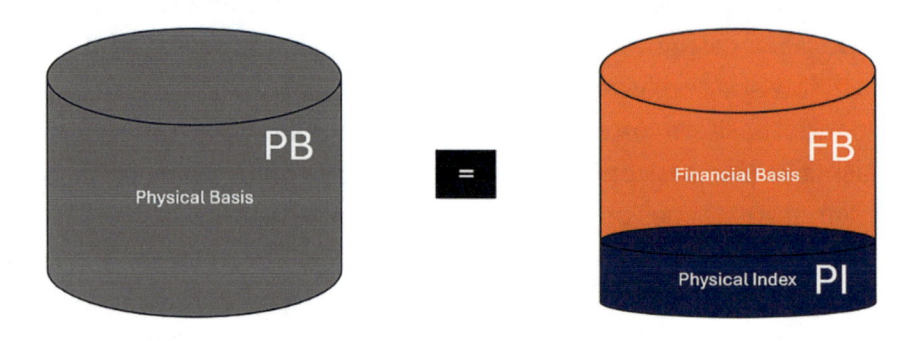

PB (Physical Basis) = FB (Financial Basis) + PI (Physical Index)

Get your trading cheat sheet here:
https://www.NatGasHub.com/TradingCheatsheet

You don't need to always draw a T-chart in your day job. You only need a T-chart one time to understand how the cashflows and risks cancel out. Once you understand how the T-chart works, from that point onward, all you need to do is memorize these three equations I showed you.

Let's say you have memorized these three equations. Now let's go through some quizzes in which if I ask you what my risk is, you should be able to answer just by using these three equations we just covered. Remember, if I buy something, then I need to sell something against it in order to be 100 percent price-hedged.

Quiz 1:

I bought Permian fixed price physical (FPP) gas and sold futures (F) against it. Am I price-hedged? If not, what is my open risk?

Answer: Equation 1 comes into play here, which states that FPP = F + FB + PI. Since I only sold F and did not sell FB or sell PI, I'm not hedged. In order to become hedged, I need to sell FB and sell PI. Hence, my open risk is I'm long Permian financial basis (FB), and I'm long Permian physical index (PI). Being long implies I have too much of it and need to get rid of it.

Quiz 2:

I bought Waha physical basis (PB), and I sold Waha physical index (PI). Am I price-hedged? If not, what is my open risk?

Answer: Equation 3 comes into play here, which states that PB = FB + PI. I bought PB and sold PI. But I did not sell FB yet. Hence, I'm not hedged. Since I need to sell FB, that means I'm long Waha financial basis (FB). Being long implies I have too much of it and need to get rid of it.

Quiz 3:

I sold Malin fixed price financial (FPF), and I bought Malin financial basis against it. Am I price-hedged? If not, what is my open risk?

Answer: Equation 2 comes into play here, which states that FPF = F + FB. I sold FPF and bought FB. But I did not buy F yet. Hence, I'm not hedged. Since I need to buy F, that means I'm short futures (F). Being short implies I have too little of it and need to find it.

Quiz 4:

Let's make things a little more complicated. I bought Rockies fixed price physical (FPP), and I sold Rockies physical basis (PB) against it. Am I price-hedged? If not, what is my open risk?

Answer: Here both equation 1 and equation 3 come into play.

Equation 1: FPP = F + FB + PI

Equation 3: PB = FB + PI

Looking at the above two equations, equation 1 can be rewritten as follows: FPP = F + PB

I bought Rockies FPP, and I sold Rockies PB. This means that I still need to sell F. Thus, I'm not hedged. Since I need to sell F, it means I have too much of it. Hence, I'm long futures.

Quiz 5:

I bought ANR fixed price physical (FPP), and I sold ANR fixed price financial (FPF) against it. Am I price-hedged? If not, what is my open risk?

Answer: Here both equation 1 and equation 2 come into play.

Equation 1: FPP = F + FB + PI

Equation 2: FPF = F + FB

Looking at the above two equations, equation 1 can be rewritten as follows: FPP = FPF + PI

I bought ANR FPP, and I sold ANR FPF. This means that I still need to sell PI. Thus, I'm not hedged. Since I need to sell PI, it means I have too much of it. Hence, I'm long ANR physical index (PI).

Some traders only trade financial instruments. They're also called "paper" traders. Hedge funds mostly trade only paper. The size of the paper market is much larger than the physical underlying market. For example, the physical gas traded at the Henry Hub location may just be around 500,000 MMBtus per day. That's the actual volume of gas molecules being exchanged and flowing on the pipes that connect into or out of HH. But the number of paper (futures) contracts traded for the same location (Henry Hub) are many hundreds or thousands of times the actual volume of physical gas traded at the same location.

Why do hedge funds trade paper and not physical? For a variety of reasons. They do not want the hassle of making or taking delivery of actual gas molecules. That would involve scheduling gas on the pipeline. The hedge fund traders see this as an unnecessary cost. Think of it this way. You like driving your car, but you hate filling it with gas. You need to fill it with gas, because it's a necessity. You would want to spend little to no time at the gas station. Similarly, a hedge fund trader wants to spend no time scheduling gas on pipelines. They'd rather just trade the paper and not have to worry about the messy job of having to track molecules on a pipeline.

Another reason is that the liquidity is much larger in the financial markets because anyone with deep pockets can trade paper. They don't ever have to be an actual energy company (like a producer or utility) to speculate in the gas markets. The way to think about it is like this: Say you and I want to bet on the outcome of a baseball game, and we make a $100 bet with each other picking our favorite teams (in my case, the Houston Astros). Let's say we each have a friend who now wants to make a new bet of their own, with the outcome based on the outcome of my bet. My friend Toby bets against your friend Samantha. Toby bets that if Jay wins, then Samatha will pay Toby $1,000. This is basically a bet on top of a bet. The total amount betted is now $1,100. Toby and Samantha may not even like baseball, they may not ever have owned a baseball glove, or they may not have ever watched a baseball game. But they can now participate in the baseball betting market via my bet.

This is how the paper natural gas markets work. Many companies who have no involvement in the business of drilling for natural gas or burning it to produce electricity can now speculate on the price of natural gas in the hopes of making a profit. But remember, we *need* these hedge fund traders. They are our insurance agents. They take the risk away from people who do not want to carry this risk. As I stated earlier, risk can't be eliminated. It can only be mitigated or transferred to someone else who is willing to take it in the hopes of making a profit. Warren Buffett is one of the biggest insurance agents in the world. In the words of Warren, "Insurers perform a societal function that subsidizes all other economic activity, enabling risks to be taken that otherwise would be shunned."

Valuing and Trading Gas Storage

In a small village nestled in the mountains, there lived a humble beekeeper named Elara. Every spring, she carefully tended to her bees, ensuring they had enough nectar to produce honey throughout the season. As summer turned to fall, she began to harvest the honey, meticulously storing it in jars for the long winter ahead. Each jar was a testament to her patience and foresight, ensuring that the village would have a sweet supply of honey even when the flowers were long gone. Elara's careful planning and resource management not only sustained her through the harshest winters but also brought prosperity to her village.

Just as Elara skillfully managed her honey storage to provide for her village, understanding the nuances of valuing and trading gas storage can yield significant benefits in the natural gas market.

In its simplest form, a storage facility can be thought of as a hole in the ground. You buy and store (natural gas) in the cheaper (shoulder) months, which are typically April and October, when gas demand is the lowest due to mild weather. It is important to dissect the different pieces that make up a storage portfolio:

1. **The storage space (the hole in the ground):** A trader leases storage space from a pipeline. This is like renting an apartment. The lease can be for any length of time. Typically, it covers at least one summer and one winter

season for a total of 365 days so that the trader has ample opportunities to make money.

2. **The physical gas:** This is the volume of natural gas that is injected at opportunistic prices into the storage facility. The storage trader has to make their best bet about when they think the gas prices have dropped low enough.

3. **The hedge:** Once the gas is purchased and injected, it then becomes a fixed price physical product. We know from equation 1 in the earlier chapter that this is the riskiest type of position to carry. Hence, the trader must sell something against the gas in ground. Equation 1 says that FPP = F + FB + PI. The trader must sell the highest price they can find (within the tenor of their storage lease contract). They will look at the forward curve for both the futures (F) price and the forward curve for the financial basis (FB) price. They will pick the highest priced months and sell the F and FB in those months. Most traders leave the physical index (PI) risk unhedged because this is very low risk. Also, the traders don't want to lock in the sale of physical molecules because they may decide to change their mind (based on changing F and FB prices). Let's say they initially sold January futures (F) and January financial basis (FB). But 15 days later, the February futures (F) and February financial basis (FB) is trading higher. They will then want to "roll" their hedges from January to February. *Rolling* means buying back one month and selling another in order to capture a higher profit.

Let's look at an example that will make this clear. We will look at high turn, high optionality storage in this example. These are the different types of combinations of a storage lease that a trader could buy in the market:

a. Low turn, low optionality
b. Low turn, high optionality
c. High turn, low optionality
d. High turn, high optionality

In order to understand how a storage trader thinks about trading storage, let's use an analogy. Let's say I'm an iPhone trader, and I want to try to make a profit buying and selling iPhones over the next one year opportunistically. I buy 1,000 iPhones and lease a public storage garage of 1,000 square feet to store my iPhones. I used my credit card to buy these iPhones, so I owe my bank monthly interest on the borrowing cost for both the iPhones and the storage facility. Let's say the storage facility owner rents to me the 1,000 square feet at $1 per square foot per month. Hence, my monthly rent is $1,000. Note that in this case, the storage facility owner will receive the $1,000 rent from me regardless of whether I make any profit on my fledgling iPhone business. This is my sunk cost.

iPhone Trading Versus Storage Trading

iPhone Trading	Storage Trading
1. Rent 1,000 Sq Ft	1. Rent 1 Bcf (1,000,000 MMBtus)
2. Rent space from Public Storage	2. Lease Storage from Egan Hub
3. Monthly Rent = $1/sf	3. Monthly Demand = $0.05/MMBtu
4. Rent Term: 1 Year	4. Lease Term: 1 Year
5. Guaranteed space	5. Firm Storage Contract
6. Entry Charge: $5/day	6. Injection Charge: $0.05/MMBtu
7. Exit Charge: $5/day	7. Withdrawal Charge: $0.05/MMBtu
8. Electricity Charge: 2% of rent	8. Fuel Charge: 2% of volume (in-kind)
9. Misc Charge: $25/month	9. ACA Charge: $0.0015/MMBtu
10. In Limit: 1,000 iphone/day	10. Daily Injection Limit: 100,000 MMBtus
11. Out Limit: 1,500 iphone/day	11. Daily Withdrawal Limit: 150,000 MMBtus
12. Sales Tax owed to local county	12. Ad Valorem Tax owed to local county
13. Can't hedge future iPhone price, no futures market	13. Hedge by selling Futures (F) + Fin Basis (FB) + Phys Index (PI)

Let's say I buy one year 1 Bcf (1,000,000 MMBtus) storage space at Egan Hub. The term of my rental lease is from April 1 of the current year to March 31 of the following year. Let's say Egan charges me $0.05/MMBtu/month (pipelines call this the reservation or demand charge). Hence, my monthly demand charge owed to the Egan Hub is $0.05/MMBtu × 1,000,000 = $50,000. I pay this each month regardless of whether I make money trading around my storage space. The pipeline rep's job is done, in that he has now earned a guaranteed payout of $50,000 per month or $600,000 selling me a one-year lease contract, regardless of whether I make or lose money as a trader over the next one year. The pipeline rep is trading his asset, which is the space on the pipeline. I'm trading my asset, which is my skill set to opportunistically make money in the market. It may appear that the pipeline rep is a better trader. They are, on day 1 of my lease contract. But think of the pipeline rep as a landlord. His income is capped. As a tenant, Apple makes a trillion dollars in the market selling their iPhones. But Apple's landlord makes a pittance compared to Apple's profits. As a trader, you must decide whether you want to be a landlord or a tenant. Low risk yields a low reward, and vice versa.

The pipeline rep also makes more money by charging me additional fees, such as an injection charge, withdrawal charge, and fuel charge. These are called variable charges. Here is how they work: Let's say on a certain day, I'm able to find cheaply priced gas in the market. I decide to inject 100,000 MMBtus into my storage space. The pipeline will charge me the following variable charges (which the pipeline and I have agreed to in advance) in addition to my monthly demand charge:

Injection Commodity Charge ($0.05/MMBtu) = 100,000 MMBtus × $0.05 = $5,000

Injection Fuel Charge (2%) = 100,000 MMBtus × 2% = 2,000 MMBtus (paid in-kind)

Paid in-kind means that the pipeline will forfeit 2 percent of the gas injected, here 2,000 MMBtus. So out of the 100,000 MMBtus I bought, only 98,000 get injected into my storage space. I'm reminded of this line from the movie *Godfather*, when Michael Corleone says, "It's not personal, Sonny. It's strictly business." This is how pipelines make profits. They are toll collectors, and they charge you each time you show up. Similarly, if I were to withdraw gas, I'd be hit with a withdrawal commodity charge and another withdrawal fuel charge. These charges can be negotiated with the Godfather before the lease term begins. But once the ink is dry, the pipeline rep doesn't care what the price of gas is in the market. They would still collect the agreed upon charges each time I inject or withdraw gas. Hence, a storage trader must have all these charges memorized. As they are watching prices move on the six different screens in front of him, they are waiting for the price of gas to rise or drop just enough so that they can still make money after paying all the pipeline charges. Another pipeline charge incurred is called the annual charge adjustment (ACA). This charge is so minuscule that most traders ignore it in their day-to-day trading decisions.

High-Turn Versus Low-Turn Storage

In this example, Egan allows me to inject 100,000 MMBtus per day and withdraw 150,000 MMBtus per day. Thus, the quickest I can fill up my storage space of 1,000,000 MMBtus (1 Bcf) is if I inject every day for 10 days straight: 100,000 MMBtus × 10 days = 1,000,000 MMBtus. Let's say I fill up my storage in 10 days. Now, to make money, I could sell the gas at a higher price than what I bought it for. Let's say that prices are high and I can sell all my gas immediately. But the pipeline only allows me to withdraw a maximum of 150,000 MMBtus per day. Thus, the soonest I can empty my storage is in 6.66 days (1,000,000 MMBtus ÷ 150,000 MMBtus/day). So, the quickest I can fill up my storage is 10 days. The quickest I can empty it is 6.66 days. Hence, to do an entire "turn" (or churn), it would take me 16.66 days. This is the quickest I can fill up and then empty my storage. Let's approximate this 16.66 days to twice per month. Recall that I leased storage space for one year. Hence, I can recycle my storage repeatedly 24 times over the course of the year. Of course, this depends on market prices cooperating with me. But theoretically, I can churn my storage 24 times per year, in this example. Anything higher than four times per year is considered "high-turn" storage. Anything less is considered "low-turn" storage.

As a trader, I would want to buy high-turn storage because it gives me more flexibility (optionality). But high-turn storage is also more expensive relative to low-turn storage. As a trader, you can decide how much risk you want to take. But how does a trader decide? Well, like anything in life, you weigh the benefits versus the costs. If you see that Apple stock price has been trading at $1,000 for the past year and suddenly it drops to $750, you may decide it's a good time to buy it. It could be Apple stock, or a BMW, a gold ring, or storage space. Some traders will use intuition (gut feeling or hair on the back of their neck), some will use their past experiences, some may use sophisticated option pricing models (more on this soon), and yet others may just view it as a lottery ticket. The point is that two traders may view the same information in the market and make opposite decisions (buy versus sell). That's what creates price volatility. Volatility is driven by human behavior. Now you know the difference between high-turn versus low-turn storage.

Some storage facilities like Egan may have multiple pipelines interconnecting with it. This creates optionality. Going back to my iPhone example, if residents in one neighborhood in my vicinity are willing to pay a higher iPhone price versus in another neighborhood, then I have an option to pick the highest. The more neighborhoods and suburbs I have access to, the more flexibility I have in selling my iPhones at the best price in the market. If my storage facility is in the middle of nowhere, then I would have to factor in the cost of driving to the nearest city to sell my iPhones. Hence, the more pipes that connect to a storage facility, the more it can charge shippers (renters) for convenience. A high-turn storage facility may only have one pipe connected to it. That makes it high-turn, low optionality. Conversely, a low-turn storage facility may have many pipes connected to it. That makes it low-turn, high optionality. By now, you've probably guessed how the available space for each of these types of facilities trades in the market.

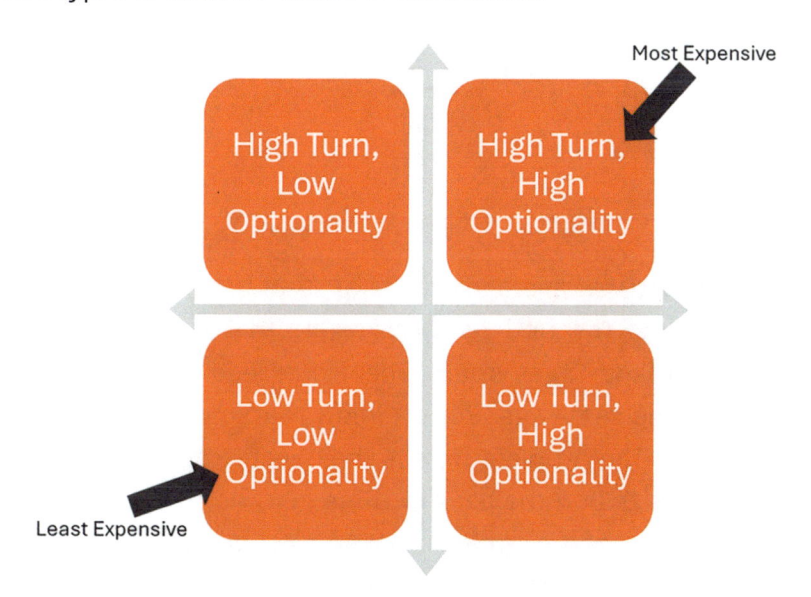

	Most Expensive
High Turn, Low Optionality	High Turn, High Optionality
Low Turn, Low Optionality	Low Turn, High Optionality

Least Expensive

Before we discuss storage trading, we need to understand the concept of volatility. The concept of volatility comes from the field of statistics. But don't cringe. We won't be delving too deep into stats. We will just use a simple example to get across the idea of volatility. In statistics, volatility is defined as the standard deviation of a group of data points. These data points could be anything: ages of people, prices of stocks, temperatures of a city, and so on. In layman's terms, volatility is defined as the average scatter around the mean.

Let's say we have a group of six people, whose ages are shown below. The mean age for this group is 29 years. Jack, Tom, and Brad are each 7 years below the mean. Paul, Sam, and Pat are each 7 years above the mean. What is the average scatter around the mean for these six people? *Scatter* is defined as how far you are from the mean.

Average scatter = (7 + 7 + 7 − 7 − 7 − 7) ÷ 6 = 0

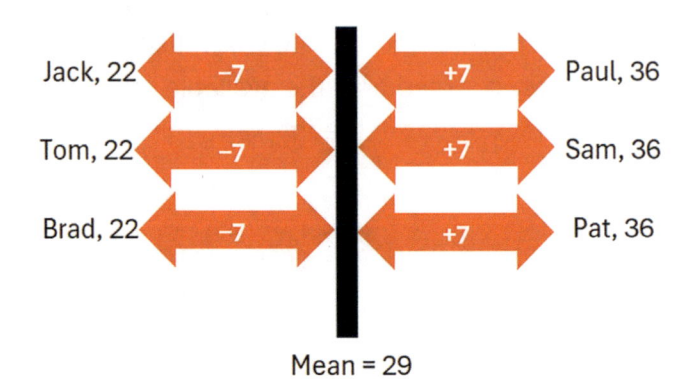

```
Jack, 22  ← −7 →  ┃  ← +7 →  Paul, 36
Tom, 22   ← −7 →  ┃  ← +7 →  Sam, 36
Brad, 22  ← −7 →  ┃  ← +7 →  Pat, 36
              Mean = 29
```

This gives us an average scatter of zero! Looking at the figure above, this doesn't sound right. This means that the volatility (average scatter) of their ages is zero. That would lead us to believe that they are all the same age. But we know that's not true. So what's the problem? The problem here is the negative sign on the ages. The positive signs on the ages of three guys negates the *negative signs* on the ages of the remaining three guys. In order to overcome this problem, we have to modify our average scatter formula. One way to do this is as follows:

Step 1: Square all the numbers. This way, we will get rid of all the negative signs.

Step 2: Then take the average.

Step 3: Take the square root. Because we squared the numbers earlier, we must take the square root at the end to undo the square in step 1.

This gives us a new formula:
Step 1: [$7^2 + 7^2 + 7^2 + (-7)^2 + (-7)^2 + (-7)^2$] ÷ 6
Step 2: [49 +49 +49 +49 +49 +49] ÷ 6 = 49
Step 3: Square root of 49 = 7 years

Hence, our standard deviation is seven years. This sounds right. Compare this to the earlier answer we got, which was zero. When you open any statistics textbook, you will see this complicated-looking scary formula for standard deviation. But worry not! The formula does exactly what we just did in the three steps above.

Formula for Standard Deviation (SD)

$$SD = \sqrt{\frac{\sum(x_i - \mu)^2}{N}}$$

Now it should be clear to you why the formula for standard deviation first squares the numbers and then takes the square root. It's all done to get rid of that pesky negative sign. Nobody likes being negative, not even a statistician!

We calculated the standard deviation of the ages of six people. You could calculate the standard deviation of any set of numbers—for example, the prices of natural gas over a seven-day period. So now that we understand standard deviation (volatility), let's discuss storage trading. Storage is basically a financial instrument called an "option" If you own a stock option, you have the right but not the obligation to buy it. Similarly, if you own storage space on a pipeline, you have the right but not the obligation to fill gas in the storage space (you exercise your option). Buying an option is the same thing as buying volatility. This is because one of the primary drivers of an option's value is the volatility of the underlying asset's price. Here, the underlying asset is the price of natural gas. More specifically, it's the difference in price of natural gas between the highest and lowest priced months. Traders will refer to buying storage as "being long vol."

Storage as a calendar spread option (CSO): A storage trader views a storage lease as a calendar spread call option. The spread is the difference in price between the lowest month (injection price) versus the highest month (withdrawal price). Let's look at an example.

In this example, we're valuing a 12-turn storage facility. This is valued as a series of 12 calendar spread options (CSOs). Each monthly CSO can be valued using a Black-Scholes option calculator. Keep in mind that we're trying to estimate the value of the storage space only (the hole in the ground), not the value of the physical gas that will get injected into it. You would input the following into your Black-Scholes CSO model:

Underlying price = $0.50/MMBtu (withdrawal price $6.50 – injection price $6.00)

Strike price = $0.2215 (injection commodity charge $0.05 + withdrawal commodity charge $0.05 + fuel charge 2% + ACA charge $0.0015)

Calculate fuel charge as 2% of injection price $6.00, which equates to $0.12.

Annualized volatility = 30%

Interest rate = 5% (use the interest rate your company's treasurer charges you)

Time to expiration = 31 days in the month

Let's say the option calculator gives you a value of $0.10 per MMBtu for this month.

Calendar spread option (CSO) value = intrinsic value + extrinsic value

Compare this to what the pipeline rep is charging you for leasing the storage space. Recall that in this example, we said the pipeline is charging you a rent (demand charge) of $0.10 per MMBtu per month. Hence, your profit in this case would be zero because the option is worth $0.10 and you paid $0.10. This is the break-even price. The option value would have to be more than this price to allow you to make a profit.

We valued this option conservatively, which is what every trader should do. But recognize that there is more value in this option than what the Black-Scholes model is telling you. Here are some additional pockets of value we didn't input into our model.

Underlying price: We used the same location to derive both the injection price and the withdrawal price. In reality, Egan Storage is connected to multiple pipelines, such as Columbia, ANR, TETCO, Trunkline, Florida Gas, and Tennessee. You would use the lowest price gas you could find on any of these pipes as your injection price. You would use the highest price gas you could find on any of these pipes as your withdrawal price. That would give you a higher profit. Since we didn't take this account when valuing the option, we know this option has some "gravy."

Strike price: There could be other charges you did not take into account, such as the ad valorem tax charge (more on this later). Every storage trader must read the fine print in the storage lease contract to avoid surprises later.

Annualized volatility: Typically, a trader would obtain the volatility quote from the option market. However, it may be very hard to obtain the volatility for the exact pipeline locations where you are injecting the gas and where you are withdrawing it. This is because not many options are traded for those locations. In this case, a trader may use the Henry Hub location as a proxy.

Valuing a natural gas calendar spread option is part science and part skill. This is where a trader's skill comes into play. A good storage trader would know whether the Henry Hub volatility needs to be dialed up or down to make it match the expected volatility of the injection and withdrawal locations. Predicting volatility is like predicting the future. Hence, this is the trader's best estimate. Think about it like trying to predict how many exact inches of rainfall would occur in The Woodlands, Texas (a suburb of Houston) in a certain month. You may have historical rainfall data for Houston, Texas, but not for The Woodlands, Texas. Thus, you would have to use Houston as a proxy for The Woodlands.

Interest rate: You should also value the option using a range of interest rates, as these could change in the future.

Every time a trader buys gas and injects it into storage, they must sell something in order to stay hedged. From our equation 1, we know that FPP = F + FB +PI. Let's say the trader buys 10,000 MMBtus of ANR Pipeline fixed price physical (FPP) gas for injection into storage today. In order to hedge their storage book, they will typically sell 10,000 MMBtus of ICE LD1 futures by picking the highest priced month on the forward futures curve (typically January or February). Let's say they sell February futures (F). This will hedge a big component of their price risk. A somewhat smaller component is comprised of the financial basis (FB). The trader would sell 10,000 MMBtus of ANR financial basis (FB). The FB trade must also be for the same month, in this case, February. The only thing left to sell is the ANR physical index. We already know why the PI is the smallest component of the risk: because it doesn't fluctuate much. Hence, the trader will usually leave this portion of the hedge open until they get closer in time to February. Leaving the PI open also allows them to "roll" (transfer) their hedge to another month in case, for instance, January runs up in price more than February.

Here is how the gas injected into storage is hedged:

Buy 10,000 MMBtus ANR fixed price physical (FPP) at $6.60
Sell 10,000 MMBtus L1D futures (F) at $6.80
Sell 10,000 MMBtus ANR financial basis (FB) at –$0.20

Once the trader injects the gas and hedges it as shown above, they are not exposed to daily price fluctuations (except for the physical index leg, which they intentionally left unhedged and which does not fluctuate much anyway).

Let's say that tomorrow, the trader does similar transactions and buys another 10,000 MMBtus at $6.70. They also hedges it the same way.

Now they have 10,000 MMBtus of gas purchased at $6.60

And they have another 10,000 MMBtus of gas purchased at $6.70

Their weighted average cost of gas (WACOG) = (10,000 × $6.60) + (10,000 × $6.70) ÷ (10,000 +10,000) = $6.65. WACOG is an accounting concept. Traders don't care much about WACOG.

Ad valorem tax: When a trader injects gas into a storage facility, in some counties, a tax is levied on the gas owner. This tax is assessed based on the value of the gas-in-ground. Since this tax is based on the value of gas, it is called an ad valorem (Latin for "according to value") tax. For example, the county may have a law that says as of December 31, if a trader has $1 million worth of gas in the ground, then the county charges a statutory tax rate of 2 percent, or $20,000, for the tax year. For most counties, the tax assessment date is either September 30 or December 31. Most traders will try to reduce their gas inventory as they are approaching this date. This is a tax-avoidance trading strategy.

For instance, let's say a trader knows he will have to pay $0.05 per MMBtu worth of taxes on September 30. On September 29, let's say the trader has an opportunity to sell gas to someone at a loss of $0.04 per MMBtu. Would you intentionally engage in a loss-making trade? Well, yes, because in this case, you will lose $0.04 on the gas trade but you will save $0.05 by not having to pay the ad valorem tax. This is a net gain of $0.01 per MMBtu. In the process, the trader also made his client happy by selling him some gas $0.04 cheaper than the rest of the market. Oddly enough, this "loss-making" trade turns out to be a win-win! It's similar to selling stocks in your portfolio at year-end in order to intentionally take some losses so that it reduces your IRS taxable income.

Valuing storage as a calendar spread option is complicated because it involves trying to estimate the volatility correctly. A lot of traders do not want to mess with the complicated concept of volatility. There is another way to value gas storage space:

Gas storage space value = intrinsic value + extrinsic value

The term *extrinsic value* comes from the world of financial derivatives. When you value any option using a model like Black-Scholes, an option is comprised of both intrinsic value and extrinsic value. Intrinsic value is the value that is derived from the price of natural gas. Extrinsic value is the value derived from factors (such as volatility) other than the underlying asset's price. Sometimes, traders will estimate only the intrinsic value of an option when they are bidding for storage space. Why would they do this? If a trader can buy storage space for the intrinsic value only, then they know they got the extrinsic value for free! This is also a conservative way to value storage. Moreover, valuing storage using price alone (versus price and volatility) is easier because prices are liquid and easily discoverable. Recall that volatility may have to be estimated by the trader. This makes valuing the extrinsic portion tricky and prone to error.

Another concept storage traders have to deal with is called storage ratchets. Ratchets are basically restrictions on how much gas can be injected or withdrawn within a certain time period. This is to preserve the structural integrity of the storage cavern. Remember, storage is a hole in the ground. The pipeline operator must be careful not to allow too many injections or withdrawals simultaneously, or else the cavern could be damaged, unusable, or worse, unsafe. This happens because all the storage traders are driven by the same price signals. If the price of gas is falling, then obviously everyone wants to inject it at the same time. This is why the storage operator (pipeline) implements ratchets. Ratchets are built into each trader's storage contract so that the trader knows beforehand what their restrictions are. Different storage facilities will have different ratchets. To give you an idea, a storage ratchet is a legal clause (restriction) that looks like this:

> In this example, we're evaluating a 1 Bcf storage lease.
> Ratchet provisions for 1 Bcf storage space:
> Summer injection season (April to October):

- By the end of April, the customer must have at least 20 percent of their total capacity (0.2 Bcf) in storage.
- By the end of July, the inventory must reach at least 50 percent of total capacity (0.50 Bcf).
- By the end of October, the customer should have injected up to 80 percent of total capacity (0.80 Bcf).

Winter withdrawal season (November to March):

- The customer must not drop below 25 percent of total capacity (0.25 Bcf) by the end of February to ensure there's sufficient gas during the peak demand of winter months.

Since ratchets are restrictions, they decrease the value of a storage contract. Hence, a storage trader must take this into account in their storage valuation model.

Let's look at an example of how to determine the intrinsic value of a gas storage lease. Remember, we are valuing the storage space alone. We are not valuing the gas that we plan to inject. Let's list the factors we need to calculate the intrinsic value of gas storage space on a pipeline:

1. Price of gas
2. Pipeline charges (injection/withdrawal fuel charge, commodity charge, and ACA charge)
3. Interest rate
4. Ad valorem tax

Here is an Excel model to calculate storage intrinsic value. Let's value the same Egan Storage contract for 1 Bcf with a 1-year tenor, which we discussed earlier. You can obtain this spreadsheet here to plug in latest prices and other variables:

https://www.NatGasHub.com/Storage

Today's Date	03/31/24	
Fuel Injection Cost	2%	
Fuel Withdrawal Cost	2%	
Commodity Injection Cost	$0.05	per MMBtu
Commodity Withdrawal Cost	$0.05	per MMBtu
ACA Cost	$0.0015	per MMBtu
Interest Rate	5%	per year
Ad Valorem Tax	2%	per year (assessed as of Dec 31st)

Month	Injection Price	Withdrawal Price	Injection Volume	Withdrawal Volume	Injection Fuel Cost	Withdrawal Fuel Cost	Injection Commodity Cost	Withdrawal Commodity Cost	ACA Cost	Total Cost	Injection Cost ($)	Withdrawal Revenue ($)	Discount Period (in years)	Discount Factor	Discounted Injection Cost Net of Costs	Discounted Withdrawal Revenue
04/01/24	$3.000	$3.090	1,000,000		($60,000)	$0	($50,000)	$0	($1,500)	($111,500)	($3,000,000)	$0	0.0833	0.9959	($3,098,875)	$0
05/01/24	$3.100	$3.250			$0	$0	$0	$0	$0	$0	$0	$0	0.1667	0.9919	$0	$0
06/01/24	$3.200	$3.300			$0	$0	$0	$0	$0	$0	$0	$0	0.2500	0.9879	$0	$0
07/01/24	$3.300	$3.380			$0	$0	$0	$0	$0	$0	$0	$0	0.3333	0.9839	$0	$0
08/01/24	$3.400	$4.000		1,000,000	$0	($80,000)	$0	($50,000)	($1,500)	($131,500)	$0	$4,000,000	0.4167	0.9799	($128,854)	$3,919,504
09/01/24	$3.350	$3.500			$0	$0	$0	$0	$0	$0	$0	$0	0.5000	0.9759	$0	$0
10/01/24	$3.250	$3.400	1,000,000		($65,000)	$0	($50,000)	$0	($1,500)	($116,500)	($3,250,000)	$0	0.5833	0.9719	($3,272,037)	$0
11/01/24	$4.000	$4.250			$0	$0	$0	$0	$0	$0	$0	$0	0.6667	0.9680	$0	$0
12/01/24	$4.500	$4.600			$0	$0	$0	$0	$0	$0	$0	$0	0.7500	0.9641	$0	$0
01/01/25	$4.750	$4.900			$0	$0	$0	$0	$0	$0	$0	$0	0.8333	0.9602	$0	$0
02/01/25	$5.000	$5.250		1,000,000	$0	($105,000)	$0	($50,000)	($1,500)	($156,500)	$0	$5,250,000	0.9167	0.9563	($149,655)	$5,020,371
03/01/25	$4.600	$4.800			$0	$0	$0	$0	$0	$0	$0	$0	1.0000	0.9524	$0	$0
04/01/25	$4.100	$4.250			$0	$0	$0	$0	$0	$0	$0	$0	1.0833	0.9485	$0	$0
			2,000,000	2,000,000	($125,000)	($185,000)	($100,000)	($100,000)	($6,000)	($516,000)	($6,250,000)	$9,250,000			($6,649,420)	$8,939,875

Valuing and Trading Gas Storage | 59

Gross Profit/Loss	$2,290,454
Ad Valorem Tax	($65,000)
Net Profit	$2,225,454
Net Profit per MMBtu per year	$0.556
Net Profit per MMBtu per month	$0.046

In the table above, you will see that it makes the most sense to inject the gas in April 2024 because the price is the cheapest. We fill up the storage at this price. Then, we empty the storage in August 2024, which is the highest price month in the summer. We repeat the same process in the winter. We have now cycled this storage facility twice (two injections and two withdrawals): once in the summer (April 2024 and August 2024), then again in the winter (October 2024 and February 2025). This is typically how often you will get to cycle the whole storage facility in a year. Traders will try to optimize this injection and withdrawal cycle throughout the year as prices move. They will constantly watch prices. If prices warrant, they may inject sooner or later or withdraw sooner or later.

This storage contract is intrinsically worth roughly $0.045 per MMBtu per month. This is my break-even price. If I can buy it for cheaper, then more profit for me! *Note that this is the intrinsic value only*. Even if I can buy it at $0.045, I know this storage facility has some extrinsic value too. I would still buy it at $0.045. I would then aggressively trade around this asset to try and extract the extrinsic value. This value extraction is usually realized in two main ways:

Cash month volatility: In the market for physical natural gas trading, the terms *cash month* and *cash trading* refer to the buying and selling of natural gas where the transactions are settled on a short-term basis, typically within a few days. This type of trading is also known as "spot trading" and involves the immediate delivery of natural gas. Cash trading usually involves the delivery of natural gas within the next day, or up to within a month. This contrasts with forward (futures) trading, where delivery might be scheduled for a date further in the future. Notice that the injection price shown in the table above for April 2024 is $3.00/MMBtu. This means that I can buy gas at $3.00 for every day in the month of April 2024. However, in reality, the price never stays constant for the whole month. In fact, there exists a daily spot or cash market as we get into the month. So on each day in the month of April 2024, there exists a tradeable market for buying and selling gas for the same day, for the next day, and for the balance-of-the-month (BalMo). Any time I'm buying gas cheaper than $3.00, I'm making more money than I had originally modeled.

Let's say I was able to find cheap gas at $2.50 on April 8, 2024. That is $0.50/MMBtu cheaper than what I had modeled my storage contract at. Let's say that on this day, I'm able to buy 50,000 MMBtus of this cheap gas. Hence, on this day, I would lock in an additional profit of $25,000! (calculated as $0.50 \times 50,000$ MMBtus). Cha-ching! This is what we mean by cash month volatility. Things break, and prices go haywire. That creates trading opportunities and profit potential. The astute traders wait for days like these. There may only be a handful of such days throughout the year. That is why you see traders glued to their six screens scouring the market for any money-making opportunities every minute of the day. When they see one, the first one to pounce gets the prize! Then we play the same game again the next day. Some summers and winters result in such extreme prices that a trader's entire year of profits could be made on five or ten trading days of the year.

As an example, this happened during the winter storm Uri in Texas in February 2021. Cash prices in some areas of Texas and Oklahoma hit anywhere from $15 to $1,000 per MMBtu! This created significant profits for those traders who had storage contracts and were able to opportunistically inject or withdraw gas into their storage accounts across the Texas and Oklahoma region during that two-week period.

Forward month volatility: When I valued my storage contract, the highest price winter month was February 2025. Let's assume I sold futures (F) for February 2025 worth 1 Bcf (1 million MMBtus). Now let's say futures prices for the month of January 2025 run up more than February 2025. In this case, I would roll my hedge from February 2025 to January 2025. I would buy back my February 2025 futures and I would sell January 2025 futures instead. This volatility in the forward months is not as pronounced as in the cash month. This is because when constraints happen in the gas market, it affects the gas for today's flow or tomorrow's flow only (that is, the cash month). The forward months are not affected as much by a localized event like a winter storm for five days in Texas. The futures price is driven off of the Henry Hub location in Erath, Louisiana. If cash price dislocations happen in other places in the country, the Henry Hub cash price may be unaffected. Hence, the futures prices are not affected as much. There are hundreds of receipt and delivery locations in the U.S. for which cash is traded.

In general, cash (spot) volatility > forward volatility.

The highest storage trading annual profit reported by the best performing trader interviewed during the making of this book was $1.2 billion. Valuing and trading gas storage is a multifaceted process involving strategic leasing, careful market analysis, and meticulous hedging. By understanding the nuances of storage facilities, physical gas management, and financial hedging, traders can optimize their strategies and maximize profits.

Valuing and Trading Gas Transport

In a bustling market square, traders from all corners of the city gathered to exchange goods. Amidst the noise and energy, a young merchant named Lila set up her modest stall. She sold handcrafted jewelry, each piece meticulously designed and made. Lila's stall was always filled with customers because she had a keen eye for recognizing value in the tiniest of details. One day, a renowned trader, Mr. Bennett, noticed her success and approached her. He admired a particular necklace but was puzzled by its price.

"How do you determine the value of this piece, Lila?" he asked.

Lila smiled. "It's not just about the materials, Mr. Bennett. It's about the craftsmanship, the time invested, and the unique design. Each aspect contributes to its worth."

Mr. Bennett nodded, realizing that valuing something involved much more than just the obvious. It was a blend of many factors, each playing a crucial role in determining its true value.

Valuing gas transport also requires understanding the many factors that drive its price.

A gas transport trade involves moving natural gas molecules from point A to point B on a pipeline. Just like storage, transport space must be leased from a pipeline by the shipper. Valuing the transport space is different from valuing the gas itself. They are two distinct transactions done with two different counterparties.

The different features of a transport contract are defined below:

Duration of contract: Contracts can be short-term or long-term, typically ranging from a few months to several years.

Pricing structure: This could include fixed fees, commodity-based fees (linked to the price of natural gas or another index), or a combination of both. The pricing might also vary based on the capacity reserved or used.

Take-or-pay commitment: Under such agreements, the buyer is obliged to pay for a minimum amount of capacity or gas, whether or not they actually use it.

Nomination procedures: This defines how shippers notify the pipeline operator of their daily gas transportation needs and any changes to these nominations.

Quality specifications: The contract stipulates the quality of natural gas that must be maintained, such as its heat content, moisture content, and the absence of contaminants.

Balancing requirements: These terms define the responsibilities for balancing the gas input into the pipeline with the output, which can include penalties for imbalances.

Force majeure: Provisions that relieve parties from fulfilling their contractual obligations under certain unforeseeable circumstances such as natural disasters or other acts of God.

Firm versus interruptible: Your transport contract can be firm or interruptible. This defines whether you will be able to flow your gas for sure or not. If it is firm, it is like having a confirmed seat on an airplane. If it's interruptible, then you are a standby passenger. Obviously, the prices for these two levels of service are different. A firm contract has a demand or reservation charge. This is your sunk cost. This is what you pay in order to buy the "firmness." An interruptible transport contract does not have a demand or reservation charge. Other charges like fuel cost, commodity cost, ACA, and any other pipeline charges are borne by both firm as well as interruptible shippers.

Primary versus secondary: In the context of interstate natural gas transportation contracts, the distinction between primary and secondary refers to the types of rights associated with the capacity on a pipeline. These terms define how the transportation capacity is allocated and used by shippers. Here's what each term generally means:

Primary rights:
- Primary rights are tied to specific, contracted paths and capacities on a pipeline. When a shipper holds primary rights, they have the guaranteed ability to transport natural gas from a specific receipt point to a specific delivery point, up to the maximum capacity specified in their contract.
- This is often associated with firm transportation contracts, where the shipper pays for a certain level of capacity regardless of actual use, ensuring that the capacity is reserved and available when needed.
- The shipper with primary rights typically enjoys higher priority in terms of service assurance, especially compared to those holding secondary rights.

Secondary rights:
- Secondary rights allow shippers to use capacity that is not being utilized by primary rights holders. These rights are generally more flexible in terms of where gas can be picked up or dropped off along the pipeline, but they do not offer the same level of assurance or priority as primary rights.
- Secondary capacity might be used when a shipper needs to transport gas outside of their primary contracted path or when additional capacity is available because primary rights holders are not using their full allocation.
- Shippers with secondary rights are subject to more fluctuations in availability and may face interruptions, especially

during periods of high demand when primary rights holders fully utilize their reserved capacities.

In-path versus out-of-path: In interstate natural gas transportation contracts, the concepts of in-path and out-of-path transportation refer to the flexibility and limitations regarding the use of pipeline capacity based on geographic or contractual constraints. Here's a detailed look at each:

In-path transportation:
- In-path transportation refers to the shipment of natural gas within the predefined paths (in this example, Louisiana to the Chicago area) as stipulated in the transportation contract. This means that the gas is moved between receipt and delivery points that lie along the primary route for which the shipper has contracted capacity.
- This type of transportation is typically straightforward in terms of contractual permissions and tariff rates because it adheres strictly to the terms set out in the contract.
- Shippers often benefit from lower rates or more favorable terms when transporting gas in-path due to the reduced complexity and lower operational burden on the pipeline system.

Out-of-path transportation:
- Out-of-path transportation occurs when natural gas needs to be transported to a destination outside of the contracted primary route. This might involve transferring gas to different pipelines or moving it to locations that are not directly along the original path specified in the contract.
- Because out-of-path transportation can require additional coordination, change in gas flow directions, and potentially increased use of the pipeline system, it often incurs higher tariffs or fees compared to in-path shipments.

- Contracts must specifically allow for out-of-path transportation, and it may be subject to availability of capacity and additional regulatory requirements.

Both in-path and out-of-path transportation options are important for shippers and pipeline operators, providing a mix of predictability and flexibility. The availability of these options helps manage the logistical challenges of distributing natural gas across various regions, accommodating changes in supply and demand, and optimizing pipeline operations.

Each of the transport features defined above can significantly impact the flexibility, cost, and reliability of natural gas transportation, and they are often carefully negotiated to meet the specific needs of the shippers and pipeline operators.

Let's compare transport trading to iPhone trading using the parameters below.

iPhone Trading Versus Transport Trading

iPhone Trading	Transport Trading
1. Rent 1,000 Sq Ft	1. Rent 25,000 MMBtu per day
2. Rent space from Public Storage	2. Lease Storage from ANR Pipeline
3. Monthly Rent = $1/sf	3. Monthly Demand = $0.10/MMBtu
4. Rent Term: 1 Year	4. Lease Term: 1 Year
5. Guaranteed space	5. Firm Storage Contract
6. Entry Charge: $5/day	6. Commodity Charge: $0.05/MMBtu
7. Electricity Charge: 2% of rent	7. Fuel Charge: 2% of volume (in-kind)
8. Misc Charge: $25/month	8. ACA Charge: $0.0015/MMBtu
9. iPhone Price in Houston	9. Receipt Location (Rec Loc): ANR Southeast
10. iPhone Price in Chicago	10. Delivery Location (Del Loc): ANR ML7
11. Can't hedge future iPhone price, no futures market	11. Hedge by buying (at Rec Loc) & selling (at Del Loc) Phys Basis

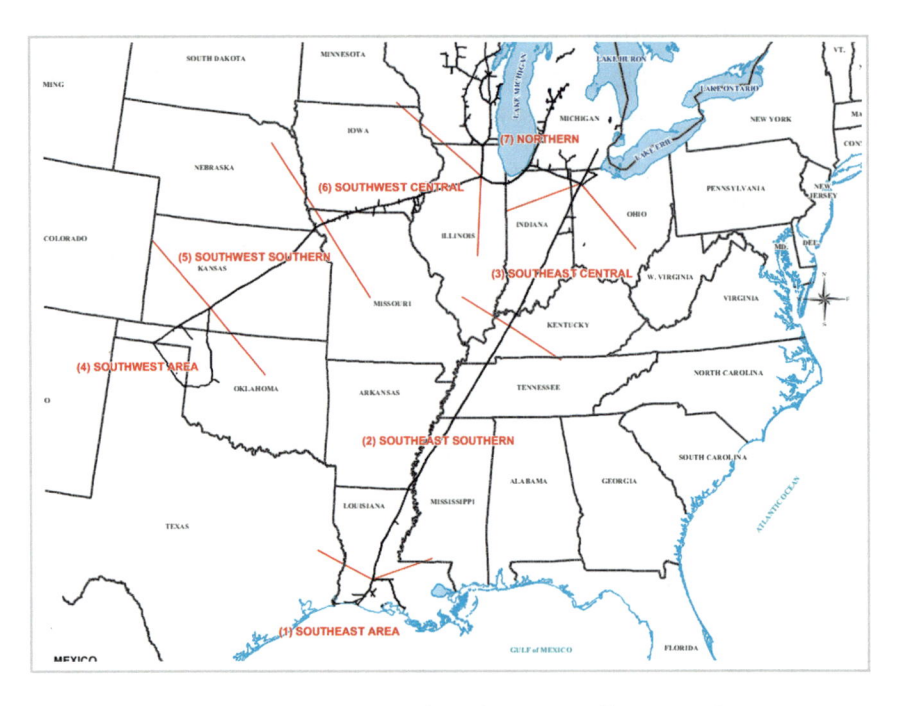

Image Source: ANR Pipeline Electronic Bulletin Board

I'm renting transport space on ANR Pipeline starting on April 1 of the current year to March 31 of the following year. I'm renting 25,000 MMBtus per day from the Southeast Zone (Louisiana area) to the ML 7 Zone (Chicago) area. I like this path because the gas in the Louisiana area can usually be purchased for cheaper than what I sell it for in the Chicago area (especially in the winter). This would be similar to buying iPhones in Houston at a cheaper price and selling them in Chicago at a premium. I will be flowing the gas from south to north and hoping that the cost to transport the gas is low enough that I can still scrape a profit when I sell the gas on the other end of the pipe in Chicago. I would need to be able to buy the gas cheap enough in Louisiana and then take into account all the charges that the pipeline will bill me to transport the gas. Then, I would need to find a buyer in Chicago who can buy gas at the highest price. Notice that the three counterparties are usually different: the person I buy the gas from in Louisiana, the ANR Pipeline from whom I'm leasing empty space on the pipeline, and the person who buys my gas in Chicago. In this example, we're valuing just the transport space that I'm buying on ANR Pipeline. Think of the pipeline as FedEx.

Let's start trading! Today is the first day that I own 25,000 MMBtus of transport space on ANR Pipeline. When I come into work today, I am watching the prices on ICE for the location ANR Southeast (ANR-SE) Head station. I'm simultaneously watching the prices on ICE for Chicago, delivered. I have my fuel and commodity costs memorized because I can't afford to waste time looking up these variable charges. Here are the variables I'm watching as I decide whether I should lock in the spread for Gas Day 1 (GD1) on my transport:

ANR Southeast Head station price on ICE, for tomorrow's flow = $3.26/MMBtu

ANR Chicago Citygate delivered price on ICE, for tomorrow's flow = $3.56/MMBtu

ANR Pipeline's commodity cost (pre-negotiated in my transport contract) = $0.145/MMBtu

ANR Pipeline fuel cost (from ANR Pipeline's tariff matrix posted on their website) = 2%

I need to convert this 2 percent to a dollar value. This is how you would do it. You take the ANR-SE price of $3.26 and multiply it by the 2 percent fuel rate. This gives me $0.0652/MMBtu. I will approximate this to $0.065 per MMBtu. I have this memorized for today's trading day. This is what I will need to pay ANR Pipeline *if* I choose to flow the gas. I will also need to pay the commodity charge of $0.145 or 14.5 ¢ per MMBtu. This gives me a total of 21 ¢ per MMBtu (14.5 ¢ + 6.5 ¢).

Now that I know what my variable charges are, I am watching prices on ICE like a hawk. ANR-SE is currently trading at $3.26 and

Chicago is trading at $3.56. This gives me a gross profit of $0.30 per MMBtu ($3.56 – $3.26). My variable costs are $0.21. This gives me a net profit of $0.09. Should I wait or lock in my profit? This is where a trader's skill comes into play. Let's say I decide to lock in my profit. I will buy 25,000 MMBtus of gas at a price of $3.26, and I will simultaneously sell 24,500 MMBtus of gas at a price of $3.56. The differing volumes are to account for in-kind fuel, which I must pay to the pipeline. Recall that the pipeline's fuel rate was 2 percent. Hence, 2 percent of 25,000 MMBtus is 500 MMBtus. This is what the pipeline will forfeit from me when I give them my gas in Louisiana. Thus, I will only be left with 24,500 MMBtus available to sell on the other end of the pipe in Chicago. I will then inform my gas scheduler of these buys and sells. My gas scheduler will then submit gas nominations to ANR pipeline. I will use my firm contract to transport this gas. I want to ensure that my profit will be realized. If I try to flow this gas on an interruptible basis, I may be cut (bumped) by another trader who has firm rights. My profit can only be realized *if and only if* the gas flows.

Notice that I did not take into account my reservation (demand) charge of $0.10 per MMBtu, which is built into my firm contract. I still need to pay this $0.10 to ANR Pipeline. Hence, my net profit is further reduced from a profit of $0.09 to a loss of $0.01. But why did I not take this $0.10 demand charge into my analysis? This is an important question every reader must understand. In the gas market, pipelines charge traders fixed charges plus variable charges.

Fixed charge, reservation, or demand cost: A trader has to pay this regardless of whether he flows the gas on the pipe or not. This is his sunk cost. Think of it as an entry fee to participate. It gives you the right to flow gas on the pipeline, but you're not obligated to flow gas. Another way to think about it is that when you buy an airline ticket, you have the right to fly but not the obligation. There may be other factors that cause you to be unable to travel. If you don't end up flying, you lose the cost of your ticket. This is the price you have to pay to have a confirmed seat, whether you fly or not.

Variable charges: These are other incremental charges a trader must pay a pipeline if and only if he decides to flow the gas. These variable charges are in addition to the fixed charges. They consist of a fuel charge (paid in-kind to the pipeline) and a commodity charge. To use the airline analogy again, this would be like baggage fees. The more bags you check, the more fees you pay. But you only pay baggage fees if you fly. Hence, the variable charges are avoidable if you don't fly.

Here's another way to think about it: Let's say you own a restaurant. Your daily rent is $2,000. That's your fixed (sunk) cost. You pay that to your landlord whether you open your restaurant tomorrow or not. You have other costs, such as hiring one cook ($100 per day) and one server ($50 per day). But these are hourly workers, and you only pay them if they work (variable charges). If you feel you will not have sufficient sales tomorrow to cover your fixed charge ($2,000 daily rent) plus the variable charges ($150 per day), then you may make the decision to keep the restaurant shut tomorrow. Let's say that you only estimate $100 in restaurant sales tomorrow. Would you then open the restaurant? What about $200 or $300? Let's say you're pretty sure that you can make $1,000 in restaurant sales tomorrow because there is a big natural gas traders seminar happening at the convention center next door to your restaurant.

There are two scenarios:

Scenario 1: Keep restaurant closed
Scenario 2: Open restaurant

Let's say you decide to keep the restaurant closed. In that case, your loss would be $2,000 (your daily rent). Now let's say you decide to open the restaurant. You pay the $2,000 daily rent plus the $150 variable charges. You get $1,000 in sales. Your net profit or loss for the day is $1,000 − $2,000 − $150 = −$1,150.

Scenario 1: Keep restaurant closed; loss is $2,000
Scenario 2: Open restaurant; loss is $1,150

Clearly, you'd be better off if you had decided to open the restaurant. The key takeaway here is that you ignore the fixed charges (in this example, the rent) because it is a sunk cost. Your responsibility as a business owner is to open the restaurant as long as you can make more than your variable charges. Anytime you do that, you're better off than not running the restaurant at all.

The same thing is true when you are a gas trader deciding whether you should flow gas or not. Ignore your sunk cost. If you're able to turn a profit by making more money than your pipeline variable costs, then you should flow the gas.

You can see this in the example below. If a trader decides not to flow the gas, then they would lose $0.10 per MMBtu. This would be the wrong decision! If they decide to flow the gas by paying variable charges, then their loss is reduced to $0.01 per MMBtu.

		SCENARIO 1	SCENARIO 2
		Trading Decision by Acknowledging Demand Cost	Trading Decision by Ignoring Demand Cost
	ANR-SE Buy Price	$3.260	$3.260
	Chicago Sell Price	$3.560	$3.560
	Gross Profit	$0.300	$0.300
FIXED CHARGE	Demand/Reservation Cost	($0.100)	
VARIABLE CHARGE	Fuel Charge 2%	($0.065)	($0.065)
VARIABLE CHARGE	Commodity Charge	($0.145)	($0.145)
	Total Charges	($0.310)	($0.210)
	Net Profit	($0.010)	$0.090

Notional Versus Mark-to-Market (MTM) Value

Let's say you are looking at one month of your transport contract, and let's assume today is the 15th day of the month. You have been flowing gas every day on this contract. Part of the contract from Gas Day 1 (GD1) to Gas Day 15 (GD15) has already flowed. This is in the past. The prices are settled (that is, not fluctuating any more). The company you bought the gas from gave you a known and fixed price. The person you sold the gas to is going to pay you a known and fixed price. This portion of your transport contract in the past is referred to as the *notional* portion of your contract. The remaining portion (balance-of-the-month or BalMo) of your contract is still open. You do not know yet what tomorrow's price will be until you execute a trade and lock in a fixed price. Hence, the BalMo portion of your contract still carries risk. This is called the mark-to-market (MTM) portion of your contract. It has a daily profit and loss (P&L) associated with it, which must be tracked every day. This is part of a trader's open risk and must be measured accurately every day to avoid unforeseen losses or missed money-making opportunities.

Gas Day	Gross Rec Loc Volume ANR South East	Fuel Loss 2%	Net Del Loc Volume ANR ML7	Rec Loc Price Per MMBtu	Del Loc Price Per MMBtu	Notional Value Realized	MTM P&L Unrealized
GD 1	(25,000)	500	24,500	$3.260	$3.460	$3,270	
GD 2	(25,000)	500	24,500	$3.270	$3.470	$3,265	
GD 3	(25,000)	500	24,500	$3.330	$3.530	$3,235	
GD 4	(25,000)	500	24,500	$3.360	$3.560	$3,220	
GD 5	(25,000)	500	24,500	$3.375	$3.575	$3,213	
GD 6	(25,000)	500	24,500	$3.390	$3.590	$3,205	
GD 7	(25,000)	500	24,500	$3.405	$3.605	$3,198	
GD 8	(25,000)	500	24,500	$3.420	$3.620	$3,190	
GD 9	(25,000)	500	24,500	$3.435	$3.635	$3,183	
GD 10	(25,000)	500	24,500	$3.450	$3.650	$3,175	
GD 11	(25,000)	500	24,500	$3.465	$3.665	$3,168	
GD 12	(25,000)	500	24,500	$3.480	$3.680	$3,160	
GD 13	(25,000)	500	24,500	$3.495	$3.695	$3,153	
GD 14	(25,000)	500	24,500	$3.510	$3.710	$3,145	
			TODAY'S DATE				
GD 15	(25,000)			($0.125)	$0.130		$6,375
GD 16	(25,000)			($0.125)	$0.130		$6,375
GD 17	(25,000)			($0.125)	$0.130		$6,375
GD 18	(25,000)			($0.125)	$0.130		$6,375
GD 19	(25,000)			($0.125)	$0.130		$6,375
GD 20	(25,000)			($0.125)	$0.130		$6,375
GD 21	(25,000)			($0.125)	$0.130		$6,375
GD 22	(25,000)			($0.125)	$0.130		$6,375
GD 23	(25,000)			($0.125)	$0.130		$6,375
GD 24	(25,000)			($0.125)	$0.130		$6,375
GD 25	(25,000)			($0.125)	$0.130		$6,375
GD 26	(25,000)			($0.125)	$0.130		$6,375
GD 27	(25,000)			($0.125)	$0.130		$6,375
GD 28	(25,000)			($0.125)	$0.130		$6,375
GD 29	(25,000)			($0.125)	$0.130		$6,375
GD 30	(25,000)			($0.125)	$0.130		$6,375
Total	(750,000)	7,000	343,000			$44,778	$102,000

NOTIONAL VALUE
Closed / Settled P&L
Rec & Del Loc prices are known and fixed
Gas has flowed

MTM VALUE
Open / Fluctuating P&L
Rec & Del Loc physical basis prices are still fluctuatin
Gas has not flowed yet

In the table above, the notional value is calculated as follows:

Notional value for GD1 = (Del Loc price × Net Del Loc volume) – (Rec Loc price × Net Rec Loc volume × –1)
= ($3.46 × 24,500) – ($3.26 × 25,000 × –1)
= +$3,270

MTM P&L is calculated as follows:

MTM P&L for GD15 = (Del Loc price – Rec Loc price) × Gross Rec Loc volume
= ($0.13 – (–$0.125)) × 25,000
= +$6,375 (profit)

Hedging Transport

When I say "hedging transport," I mean hedging the space you rented on the pipeline, not the gas that flows on the pipeline. The transport space that you lease on any pipeline can be valued as a locational spread: that is, the price difference between the receipt location and the delivery location. Just like storage, transport is also a spread option. Whereas storage is a calendar spread option, transport is a basis spread option. When you buy space for storage or space for transport on any pipeline, you are buying an option contract. It's called an "option" because you have the right to inject (if it's storage) or flow (if it's transport) the gas but not the obligation. Both storage and transport options have a sunk cost (demand or reservation cost). Here is a comparison of storage versus transport:

	STORAGE	TRANSPORT
SIMILARITIES	Renting space from a pipeline	Renting space from a pipeline
	Rent a hole in the ground	Rent a Roadway from Point A to Point B
	Calendar Spread Option	Locational (Basis) Spread Option
	Has Intrinsic + Extrinsic Value	Has Intrinsic + Extrinsic Value
	Fixed Term. e.g., 1 Year	Fixed Term. e.g., 1 Year
	Daily Demand Charge (e.g., $0.05/MMBtu)	Daily Demand Charge (e.g., $0.05/MMBtu)
	Daily Fuel Charge (e.g., 2%)	Daily Fuel Charge (e.g., 2%)
	Daily Commodity Charge (e.g., $0.03/MMBtu)	Daily Commodity Charge (e.g., $0.03/MMBtu)
	Could be Firm or Interruptible	Could be Firm or Interruptible
	ACA Charge Applies (e.g. $0.0015/MMBtu)	ACA Charge Applies (e.g. $0.0015/MMBtu)
	Daily Injection Limit	Daily Transport Limit
	Can be resold to another shipper	Can be re-sold to another shipper
DIFFERENCES	Has Ad Valorem Charge	Not applicable
	Has Injection/Withdrawal Location	Has Receipt/Delivery Locations
	Has Inj/Withdrawal Charges	Not applicable
	Has Ratches	Not applicable
	Hedged by Futures (F) + Financial Basis (FB) + Physical Index (PI)	Hedged by Financial Basis (FB) + Physical Index (PI)

Since a transport contract is a spread option, it has both intrinsic and extrinsic value. We defined these concepts of intrinsic value and extrinsic value in the chapter on storage valuation. The idea is the same when valuing transport. Let's value the intrinsic portion of a transport contract first.

Today's Date	03/31/24	
Demand/Reservation	$ 0.10	per MMBtu
Transport Volume/Day	25,000	
Fuel Injection Cost	2%	
Commodity Cost	$0.05	per MMBtu
ACA Cost	$0.0015	per MMBtu
Interest Rate	5%	per year

Month	Futures (F) Price	Receipt Location Physical Basis (PB) Price (ANR-SE)	Delivery Location Physical Basis (PB) Price (ANR-ML7)	Receipt Location Fixed Price Physical (FPP) ANR-SE	Gross Profit ($/MMBtu)	Fuel Cost ($/MMBtu)	Commodity Cost ($/MMBtu)	ACA Cost	Total Cost	Net Profit ($/MMBtu)	# of Days in month	Monthly Volume	Net Profit ($)	Discount Period (in years)	Discount Factor	Discounted Net Profit ($)	Reservation Cost	Discounted Reservation Cost	Discounted Profit/Loss
04/01/24	$3.050	($0.155)	$0.100	$2.895	$0.255	($0.058)	($0.050)	($0.0015)	($0.1094)	$0.1456	30	750,000	$109,200	0.0833	0.9959	$108,757	($75,000)	($74,696)	$34,061
05/01/24	$3.230	($0.155)	$0.100	$3.075	$0.255	($0.062)	($0.050)	($0.0015)	($0.1130)	$0.1420	31	775,000	$110,050	0.1667	0.9919	$109,159	($77,500)	($76,872)	$32,286
06/01/24	$3.280	($0.155)	$0.100	$3.125	$0.255	($0.063)	($0.050)	($0.0015)	($0.1140)	$0.1410	30	750,000	$105,750	0.2500	0.9879	$104,468	($75,000)	($74,091)	$30,377
07/01/24	$3.520	($0.120)	$0.180	$3.400	$0.300	($0.068)	($0.050)	($0.0015)	($0.1195)	$0.1805	31	775,000	$139,888	0.3333	0.9839	$137,631	($77,500)	($76,250)	$61,381
08/01/24	$3.630	($0.125)	$0.190	$3.505	$0.315	($0.070)	($0.050)	($0.0015)	($0.1216)	$0.1934	31	775,000	$149,885	0.4167	0.9799	$146,869	($77,500)	($75,940)	$70,928
09/01/24	$3.570	($0.130)	$0.180	$3.440	$0.310	($0.069)	($0.050)	($0.0015)	($0.1203)	$0.1897	30	750,000	$142,275	0.5000	0.9759	$138,846	($75,000)	($73,193)	$65,654
10/01/24	$3.515	($0.160)	$0.170	$3.355	$0.330	($0.067)	($0.050)	($0.0015)	($0.1186)	$0.2114	31	775,000	$163,835	0.5833	0.9719	$159,238	($77,500)	($75,325)	$83,912
11/01/24	$3.556	($0.130)	$0.230	$3.426	$0.360	($0.069)	($0.050)	($0.0015)	($0.1200)	$0.2400	30	750,000	$179,985	0.6667	0.9680	$174,225	($75,000)	($72,600)	$101,625
12/01/24	$3.720	($0.125)	$0.260	$3.595	$0.385	($0.072)	($0.050)	($0.0015)	($0.1234)	$0.2616	31	775,000	$202,740	0.7500	0.9641	$195,455	($77,500)	($74,715)	$120,740
01/01/25	$3.934	($0.110)	$0.280	$3.824	$0.390	($0.076)	($0.050)	($0.0015)	($0.1280)	$0.2620	31	775,000	$203,066	0.8333	0.9602	$194,975	($77,500)	($74,412)	$120,563
02/01/25	$4.059	($0.100)	$0.310	$3.959	$0.410	($0.079)	($0.050)	($0.0015)	($0.1307)	$0.2793	28	700,000	$195,524	0.9167	0.9563	$186,972	($70,000)	($66,938)	$120,034
03/01/25	$4.118	($0.090)	$0.320	$4.028	$0.410	($0.081)	($0.050)	($0.0015)	($0.1321)	$0.2779	31	775,000	$215,404	1.0000	0.9524	$205,146	($77,500)	($73,810)	$131,337
04/01/25	$4.024	($0.160)	$0.240	$3.864	$0.400	($0.077)	($0.050)	($0.0015)	($0.1288)	$0.2712	30	750,000	$203,415	1.0833	0.9485	$192,942	($75,000)	($71,139)	$121,804
													$2,121,016			$2,054,683	($987,500)	($959,981)	$1,094,702

The intrinsic value of this transport is $1,094,702.

You can download this Excel spreadsheet for valuing any transport by plugging in latest prices and other variables here:

https://www.natgashub.com/Transport

In this example, we're valuing a 12-month transport lease. This is valued as a series of 12 basis spread options. Each monthly spread option can be valued using a Black-Scholes option calculator. Keep in mind that we're trying to estimate the value of the transport space only, not the value of the physical gas that will flow on this transport contract. You would input the following into your Black-Scholes spread option model:

- Underlying price spread = $0.30/MMBtu (for example, delivery price at Chicago – receipt price in Louisiana)
- Strike price = $0.2115 (fuel charge $0.065 + commodity charge $0.145 + ACA charge $0.0015)
- Annualized volatility = 30 percent (for example)
- Interest rate = 5 percent (for example, use the interest rate your company's treasurer charges you)
- Time to expiration = 31 days in the month (for example)

Let's say the option calculator gives you a value of $0.20 per MMBtu for this month:

Basis spread option model value = intrinsic value + extrinsic value = $0.30 per MMBtu

SCENARIO 1

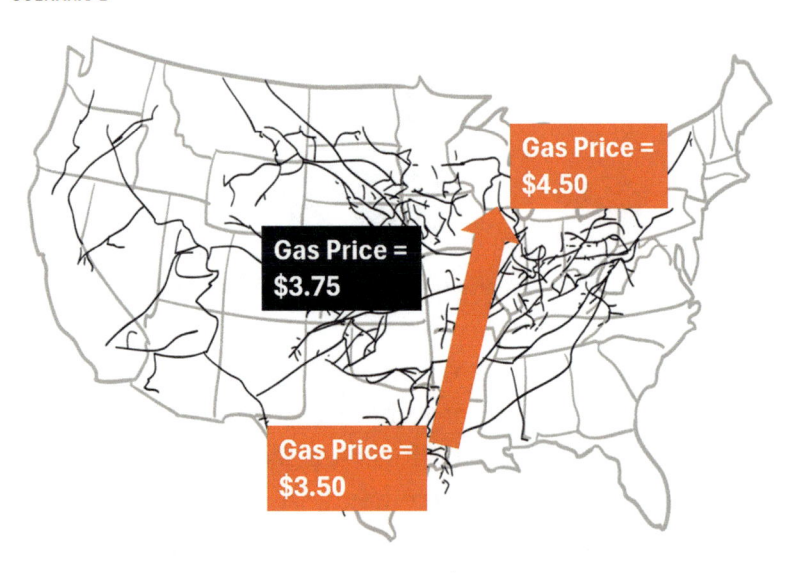

Gas Price = $4.50

Gas Price = $3.75

Gas Price = $3.50

SCENARIO 2

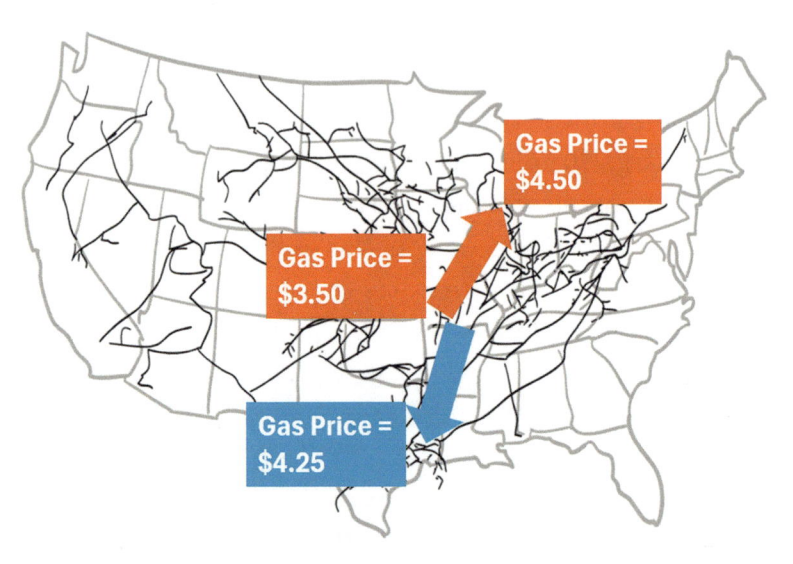

Gas Price = $4.50

Gas Price = $3.50

Gas Price = $4.25

Compare this to what the pipeline rep is charging you for leasing the transport space. Recall that in this example, we said the pipeline is charging you a rent (demand charge) of $0.10 per MMBtu per month. Thus, your profit in this month would be $0.20/MMBtu because the option is worth $0.30 and you paid $0.10. In order to calculate the extrinsic value only, you would need to know what the intrinsic value of this transport is. Recall that we already calculated the intrinsic value of this option earlier in this chapter. Armed with both intrinsic and extrinsic values, a trader would feel more comfortable bidding on this transport contract. The more accurate and reliable a trader's price and volatility quotes are that they feed into the option pricing model, the more confidence it will give them when bidding against other traders in acquiring this transport at an attractive price.

Segmentation: This a concept implemented by many traders to extract greater value from their transport space. It is the practice of chopping or splitting up your transport space into two or more segments and trading them separately. Let's say a trader owns gas transport on ANR Pipeline, which runs from Louisiana to Illinois. The two scenarios below will give you an idea of how segmentation works. The decision to chop or not chop up your transport space is based on market prices.

In scenario 1 above, the entire piece of transport space from south to north is treated as one piece because the prices in the south are the lowest of the transport and the prices in the north are the highest. So, to maximize profit, you would buy all the gas in the south and flow it all northward.

In scenario 2 above, the prices in the market are such that the cheapest price gas is available in the middle of the country. Therefore, you would buy all your gas in the middle and flow half of it northward and half of it southward. This way, you are doubling and maximizing your profit. If you don't segment, you'd be leaving money on the table.

The highest transport trading annual profit reported by the best-performing trader interviewed during the making of this book was $1.6 billion. Understanding the complexities of gas transport valuation is crucial for optimizing profits and managing risks. By considering each contract's features, traders can make informed decisions, ensuring efficient and cost-effective natural gas transportation.

Reselling storage or transport space: If a trader doesn't need the storage space or the transport space that they already own, they could resell this space to another trader. This is similar to subletting your rental office space if you have extra space in a certain month. This secondary market for trading storage or transport is a great place to find deals that could help you make more money. But where do you find these deals? They're not on Craigslist. You can find them here:

https://natgashub.com/capacity/

More information about this trading strategy can be found in the chapter titled "Ten for Ten: Ten Trading Strategies to Make You $10 Million per Year."

Valuing and Trading a Gas Park or Loan

In a bustling marketplace, a seasoned trader named Marcus encountered a shrewd merchant offering a peculiar deal. "Store my goods now, and in a few months, retrieve them for a profit," the merchant proposed. Intrigued, Marcus agreed and carefully tracked the market's fluctuations. Months later, when demand peaked, Marcus sold the goods at a significant profit, sharing the earnings with the merchant. This successful venture taught him a valuable lesson: timing and strategic partnerships are the keys to thriving in the ever-changing world of trade.

A park or loan (PAL) transaction involves the concepts of "time value of money" as well as lending and borrowing.

A gas park transaction is defined as one in which a trader buys gas and stores it with the pipeline in one month and then receives it back from the pipeline in a future month.

A gas loan transaction is defined as one in which a trader borrows gas from a pipeline and sells it in one month. They return the gas back to the pipeline in a future month.

Both the trader and the pipeline make money on each park or loan transaction. The pipeline engages in these transactions if it has too much or too little gas in any given month in order to maintain reliability (for example, in peak summer or peak winter months) as well as smooth system operations.

Let's look at a gas park transaction first. The pipeline rep will know in which months they need extra gas. They will then reach out to traders in the market via instant messaging. Pipeline reps will typically wait until the spreads are wide enough before they engage in these transactions. A spread is defined as a difference in gas prices across two months. Here are some examples of spread levels:

Cash month May 2024 ($3.15) to January 2025 ($4.20):
This implies a spread of +$1.05.

October 2024 ($3.75) to January 2025 ($4.20):
This implies a spread of +$0.45.

March 2025 ($4.45) to January 2025 ($3.10):
This implies a negative spread of –$1.35

Pipeline reps will look to historical spread levels to decide whether the current spread levels have peaked or not. Let's assume the pipeline rep needs gas in January 2025 (due to winter demand), and let's assume today is May 11, 2024. Cash for tomorrow's flow (that is, May 12, 2024) is very weak in the Gulf region and is trading at $3.15/MMBtu. The price for January 2025 futures is currently trading at $4.20. This implies a price spread of $1.05/MMBtu. I agree to park gas at the Bobcat Pipeline facility. The Bobcat rep and I agree to a profit sharing deal of 20 percent for me and 80 percent for him to execute a park transaction volume of 500,000 MMBtus. The pipeline rep usually gets the lion's share of the spread because the gas is being parked at his facility. Without the pipeline asset, I would not be able to do this type of transaction. The pipeline reps know this and use it to their advantage.

The park and loan game is really a "cost of capital" game. The trader with the lowest cost of capital usually ends up being the winner in a park or loan transaction. Let's understand why the cost of capital is so important. In order to park 500,000 MMBtus of gas tomorrow, I need to buy that much gas in the market. I am able to find all the 500,000 MMBtus on TETCO Pipeline, which interconnects with Bobcat. I buy this gas at $3.15 as fixed price physical (FPP). In order to hedge this purchase, I need to sell something. We recall equation 1:

Fixed price physical (FPP) = futures (F) + financial basis (FB) + physical index (PI)

This means that in order to be price-hedged, I need to sell F, FB, and PI. Here are my transaction prices for these legs:

Sell 500,000 MMBtus of January 2025 futures at $4.20

Sell 500,000 MMBtus of January 2025 TETCO financial basis at +$0.03

Sell 500,000 MMBtus of January 2025 physical index at +$0.005

On January 1, 2025, I will start delivering the 500,000 MMBtus to the company I sold the gas to. This is usually delivered ratably (that is, in an equal volume per day throughout the month). In this example, the 500,000 MMBtus would be divided over a period of 31 days to give me a daily volume of 16,129 MMBtus per day. The pipeline rep will allow me to withdraw (unpark) this gas from the pipeline's storage cavern so I can sell it in the market. Notice how this transaction is similar to a storage withdrawal transaction. In fact, a park or loan transaction is quite similar to a storage injection or withdrawal transaction. Both involve parking or injecting gas in one month. Both involve loaning or withdrawing gas in another month. The biggest difference between a park or loan versus a storage deal is that the park or loan transaction falls under an interruptible rate schedule, whereas a storage deal usually involves firm injections or withdrawals.

Note: A storage contract can be either firm or interruptible. A park or loan contract is almost always interruptible.

Now let's put all these park transactions on a T-chart:

	1 Buy Trade, 3 Sell Trades	
	BUY	SELL
1. FIXED PRICE PHYSICAL (FPP)	($3.150)	
2. FUTURES (F)		L1D $4.20
3. FINANCIAL BASIS (FB)		Tetco IFERC L1D + $0.03
4. PHYSICAL INDEX (PI)		Tetco IFERC + $0.005
	($3.150)	$4.235
		$1.085 Profit/Loss (Before Cost of Capital)

The potential profit on this park transaction is $1.085 per MMBtu. All the transactions shown on the T-chart above can be transacted by any trader in the market. So how does a pipeline rep decide with which trader to do this deal? The only differentiating factor among traders is the cost of capital. The profit of $1.085 above does not take into account my cost of capital. The cost of capital comes into play because I have to buy all this gas to park it at Bobcat. Since I (versus the pipeline rep) am the one buying the gas, I need to take into account my cost of capital. I have to borrow money from my company treasurer to buy all this gas. If I work for a bank, then my cost of capital is cheap. Thus, I will be able to buy 500,000 MMBtus of gas at a cheaper price than another trader in the market. Conversely, if I work for a small private company, my cost of capital will be quite high, and I may not be able to compete with a big bank.

Let's say my treasurer tells me that my cost of capital is 4 percent per year. I need to convert this percentage into a dollar per MMBtu basis. This is how a trader would calculate his cost of capital. In this example, the cost of capital is the interest cost that trader is paying to buy this gas at $3.15 per MMBtu. If they wanted to park this gas for a period of one year, then they would need to pay an interest charge to his treasurer of 4 percent on the $3.15 price, which is equivalent to $0.126 per MMBtu. I'm calculating simple interest for simplicity. In reality, traders use compound interest. However, this park transaction is not for one year. It is for the time period of May 24, 2024 through January 31, 2025 (252 days). I need to convert my annual cost of capital from 365 days to 252 days.

Cost of capital for 252 days = cost of capital for 365 days × (252 ÷ 365)

= 4% × (252 ÷ 365)

= 2.762%

Since the gas purchase price is $3.15/MMBtu, my cost of capital is $3.15 × 2.762% = $0.087/MMBtu.

Gas Purchase Price	$ 3.150	
Park Date	05/24/24	
Park Payback Date	01/31/25	
Tenor	252	Days
Cost of Capital	4.000%	per 365 days
Cost of Capital	2.762%	per 252 days
Cost of Capital	$ 0.087	

I would let the pipeline rep know that this is my cost of capital. The pipeline rep would then try to figure out which trader in the market has the lowest cost of capital. Let's say it ends up being me. In that case, the pipeline rep would award this deal to me. The net profit (after cost of capital) would be as follows:

Net profit (after cost of capital) = gross profit (before cost of capital) − cost of capital

= $1.085 − $0.087

= $0.998/MMBtu

Let's assume there were no brokers involved in this transaction. If there was a broker, a trader would also need to subtract broker costs from the profit. Typically, brokerage costs (referred to by traders as "bro") are small (around $0.00025 per MMBtu).

Net profit (in dollar terms) = $0.998 × 500,000 MMBtus

= $499,000

The pipeline rep's profit share is 80 percent. This means they would be paid $399,200, and I would make a $99,800 profit. Not too shabby for 30 minutes of work! The profit-share payment date is mutually agreed upon. As you can see, doing a park transaction is very lucrative for both the trader and the pipeline rep. It is fully price-hedged. Both traders and pipeline reps love doing these types of deals. Pipeline reps avoid doing too many parks or loans with the same trader even though that trader may have the lowest cost of capital. This is to avoid giving the appearance of favoritism, lest a regulator should take notice. It is also to diversify their risk so that they do not have all their eggs in one basket. For example, if this trader's company were to go bankrupt before January 2025, then the pipeline rep would be stuck with 500,000 MMBtus of extra gas that he may have to unload at a loss. Pipeline reps are also constrained by how much open space they have available to park the gas. This limits the number of parks or loans that can be done each year across all North American pipes.

Traders must stay vigilant to avoid missing opportunities. When I was trading, at times, I was frustrated at having missed a lucrative park or loan opportunity. Since I was working at JPMorgan, my cost of capital was one of the lowest in the market. But sometimes I was not aware that a park or loan opportunity existed or was being offered by some pipeline rep in the market. These PAL opportunities are not posted on any exchange or on any pipeline's website. In order to overcome this problem, I created the gTRAN product so that every trader in the market has a fair shot at participating in a PAL transaction. More info about this product can be found here:

https://natgashub.com/gTRAN/

A Gas Loan Transaction

Now let's understand a gas loan transaction and how it is structured and valued. A loan is the opposite of a park transaction.

In a park transaction, you buy the gas in the first month or leg and store it with the pipeline. Then you withdraw and sell it in the market in the second month or leg after getting it back from the pipeline.

In a loan transaction, you withdraw (borrow) the gas from the pipeline and simultaneously sell the gas in the market in the first month or leg. Then you buy and park (return and repay) it back in the second month or leg.

Let's go through an example to understand how a loan transaction works. We will look at a loan transaction involving Mississippi Hub (which is connected to Sonat Pipeline). Mississippi Hub (MH) will loan me 500,000 MMBtus of gas now. I will pay it back later. Since a loan involves borrowing gas and selling it in the market, you may have accurately predicted that the first month or leg of the loan transaction would be priced higher than the second month or leg. This is because a loan only makes sense if a trader could sell high and buy low.

Let's assume today is May 12, 2024. The MH Pipeline rep realizes that they have too much gas this month (probably because a lot of traders injected gas into storage). The MH rep wants to get rid of some gas. They would like to get all the gas back in May 2025 (before the summer demand picks up). So now we're looking at loaning gas in May 2024 versus payback in May 2025. Assume I will loan (borrow) 500,000 MMBtus of gas from MH Pipeline for tomorrow's flow date, May 13. Let's assume Sonat cash for tomorrow is trading at $3.96/MMBtu. The May 2025 futures contract is trading at $3.01/MMBtu. The Sonat basis is trading at +$0.05/MMBtu. I can also see Sonat Index for May 2025 trading at flat (that is, IFERC + $0.000). I will sell the 500,000 MMBtus of Sonat in the cash (spot) market for delivery tomorrow. As always, since I sold something, I must buy something to stay price-hedged. We know from equation 1 that FPP = F + FB + PI. I sold FPP. Hence, I need to buy F, buy FB, and buy PI. I proceed to buy 500,000 MMBtus of the May 2025 futures contract. I will also buy 500,000 MMBtus of the May 2025 Sonat financial basis at +$0.05/MMBtu. Finally, I will buy 500,000 MMBtus of the May 2025 Sonat physical index. Let's put all these transaction on a T-chart to see how the profit shakes out.

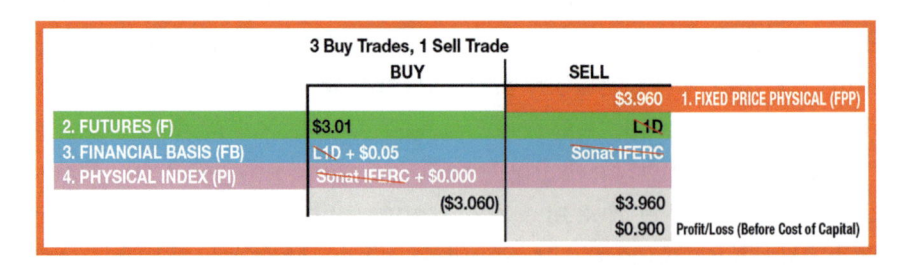

	3 Buy Trades, 1 Sell Trade		
	BUY	SELL	
		$3.960	1. FIXED PRICE PHYSICAL (FPP)
2. FUTURES (F)	$3.01	L1D	
3. FINANCIAL BASIS (FB)	L1D + $0.05	Sonat IFERC	
4. PHYSICAL INDEX (PI)	Sonat IFERC + $0.000		
	($3.060)	$3.960	
		$0.900	Profit/Loss (Before Cost of Capital)

    The profit on this loan transaction (as can be seen in the T-chart above) is $0.90/MMBtu. But this is before taking into account the cost of capital and broker costs (if any). Let's assume there were no brokers involved in this loan transaction. If there was a broker, a trader would also need to subtract broker costs from the profit. Typically, brokerage costs (referred to by traders as "bro") are small (around $0.00025 per MMBtu).

    Just like a park transaction, a loan transaction is also won or lost by the trader with the lowest cost of capital. But in a loan transaction, a trader is selling gas (not buying) in the first month or leg. This is where a loan is different from a park. Because the trader is selling first, they will receive (not borrow) the money for the gas. The trader will repay this money 383 days later. The trader can deposit this money in a bank and earn interest for 383 days. This is an added benefit and increases the profit on the loan transaction even further. Since the trader earns interest, the pipeline rep will want a chunk of the interest earnings too. I'm reminded of the Godfather scene again! After all, the gas belongs to the pipeline rep. Let's say the trader can earn 6 percent interest per annum if he deposits the gas sale proceeds in a bank. I need to convert this interest earned from 365 days to 383 days. For simplicity, I will use simple interest instead of compound interest:

Interest earned for 383 days = interest earned for 365 days × (383 ÷ 365)

= 6% × (383 ÷ 365)

= 6.296%

Since the gas sales price is $3.96/MMBtu, my interest earned is $3.96 × 6.296% = $0.249/MMBtu.

Gas Sale Price	$ 3.960	
Park Date	05/13/24	
Park Payback Date	05/31/25	
Tenor	383	Days
Cost of Capital	6.000%	per 365 days
Cost of Capital	6.296%	per 365 days
Cost of Capital	($0.249)	cost is negative for a gas loan

Net profit (after interest earned) = gross profit (before interest earned) + interest earned

= $0.90 + $0.249

= $1.149/MMBtu

Net Profit (in dollar terms) = $1.149 × 500,000 MMBtus

= +$574,500

Let's assume that in this case, the pipeline rep's profit share is 80 percent. This means they would be paid $459,600, and I would make a $114,900 profit. Pretty swell for 30 minutes of work! The profit-share payment date is mutually agreed upon. As you can see, doing a loan transaction is also very lucrative for both the trader and the pipeline rep. It is fully price-hedged. Both traders and pipeline reps love doing these types of deals. Not only does this lead to mutual profit generation for both the trader and the pipeline rep, but it also creates flexibility by reducing the gas in the storage cavern when it becomes too full. Conversely, a park transaction would increase the gas in the storage facility when the pipeline's inventory gets too low. Hence, park or loan transactions promote system reliability and flexibility. They're a win-win for the trader and the pipeline.

There is one more important concept to cover for parks or loans: interest rate risk, also known as "rho" risk. *Rho* is a letter of the Greek alphabet that is commonly used in finance to represent this risk. A trader's profit or loss is sensitive to changes in interest rates. The trader has hedged the gas prices in both legs or months of the park or loan transaction. However, the interest rate risk has not been hedged. Hedging interest rate risk is accomplished by buying and selling interest rate swaps or futures contracts. In a park or loan transaction, the pipeline rep is not exposed to any interest rate risk. They are simply guaranteed a payment (profit share) on a certain date by the trader. Regardless of what happens to interest rates, the pipeline rep will receive that fixed payment, thus insulating the rep from interest rate risk. This is a risk that must be managed and hedged by the trader alone. Very often, this risk goes unhedged because most gas traders are not familiar with how to hedge this risk. As I said earlier, not hedging is the same as speculating. You may have hedged your gas price risk. But by not hedging interest rate risk, the trader is potentially exposing themself to a bigger risk.

Why is the trader exposed to interest rate risk? The trader's treasurer is quoting them an interest rate that is valid for today. The treasurer themself is at the mercy of the interest rate market. Most trading companies have a credit trading facility (that is, a short-term loan) that is like a home equity line of credit with a floating interest rate. Tomorrow, the interest rates could rise or fall.

This exposes the trader to interest rate risk just like a homeowner is exposed to floating mortgage rate risk.

Let's look at the park transaction first. The trader is buying gas first and storing it with the pipeline for a year. They had to borrow money from his treasurer to buy this gas. In our park example, we assumed that the interest rate on the date the trader executed the park transaction was 4 percent. Let's say tomorrow the interest rate runs up to 4.5 percent. Now the trader will have to pay more in interest cost for the same park transaction they did yesterday. This extra 0.5 percent on interest cost eats into the trader's profit. They thought they had locked in his profit 100 percent. But in reality, a rising interest rate would erode profits. If the trader is lucky, the interest rates could fall and benefit the trader too. However, in trading, luck is not a good strategy. If a trader wants to speculate on rising or falling rates, then they don't need to do a park transaction for this. They can simply bet on interest rate futures.

Similarly, in a loan transaction, the trader sells gas first. They deposit the money into the bank and earn interest. If interest rates fall, he will earn less interest, which will erode the profits on his loan transaction. Worse still, they have promised to pay the pipeline rep a fixed payment resulting from interest earned, which the trader will still be on the hook for. If interest rates move a lot, it could wipe out the trader's entire profit on the deal and then some. Yet they would still have to pay the pipeline rep the fixed promised dollar amount. You can see how this deal could turn into a money loser quickly.

In order to hedge interest rate risk, a trader must first be able to quantify it. In order to do this, a trader must list all park or loan inflows and outflows as shown in the table below. These inflows and outflows must be listed in both MMBtus and also in dollar terms.

Volume (in MMBtus)	1-Jan	1-Feb	1-Mar	1-Apr	1-May	1-Jun	1-Jul	1-Aug	1-Sep	1-Oct	1-Nov	1-Dec
Park #1		(500,000)								500,000		
Park #2			(1,000,000)		500,000			1,000,000				
Loan #1	500,000					(475,000)						
Loan #2		475,000										
Loan #3			1,000,000						(1,000,000)			
Park#3				(750,000)				750,000				
Total	500,000	(25,000)	0	(750,000)	(500,000)	(475,000)	0	1,750,000	(1,000,000)	500,000	0	0

Cashflows	1-Jan	1-Feb	1-Mar	1-Apr	1-May	1-Jun	1-Jul	1-Aug	1-Sep	1-Oct	1-Nov	1-Dec
Park #1		($1,650,000)								$1,720,000		
Park #2			($2,900,000)		$1,545,000			$3,170,000				
Loan #1	$1,625,000					($1,467,750)						
Loan #2		$1,472,500										
Loan #3			$3,170,000						($3,160,000)			
Park#3				($2,377,500)				$2,475,000				
Total	1,625,000	(177,500)	270,000	(2,377,500)	(1,545,000)	(1,467,750)	0	5,645,000	(3,160,000)	1,720,000	0	0

	1-Jan	1-Feb	1-Mar	1-Apr	1-May	1-Jun	1-Jul	1-Aug	1-Sep	1-Oct	1-Nov	1-Dec
Interest Rate	4.25%	4.50%	4.75%	4.35%	4.80%	4.90%	5.10%	5.35%	5.45%	5.60%	5.80%	6.00%
DV01	$ 123	$ (139)	$ 178	$ (217)	$ (316)	$ (451)		$ 668	$ (714)	816		

The table above shows three park transactions and three loan transactions. For example, park 1 shows the trader is parking 500,000 MMBtus in the month of February and withdrawing 500,000 in the month of October. The corresponding cashflows for park 1 are $1,650,000 in February and $1,720,000 in October. The cashflows are derived from the prices at which the trader agreed to execute the two legs of the park transaction with that pipeline rep. Similarly, all the volumes and cashflows for the other parks and loans are laid out in the table above. The next thing is to obtain the interest rate curve from the market. This is readily available information on the internet. The final variable to calculate is known as "DV01" (pronounced as Dee-Vee-Oh-One). This is defined as the dollar value of one basis point:

1 BASIS POINT = 0.01%

This measures how sensitive to change the trader's cashflows are (in U.S. dollar terms) in each month if U.S. interest rates change by one basis point (that is, 0.01 percent) in that month.

DV01 is a slightly complicated calculation and is usually automatically performed by the trader's energy trading and risk management (ETRM) system. The formula for DV01 is shown below:

$$\text{DV01} = -P \times \frac{\Delta P}{\Delta y}$$

where:

- P is the current price of the bond.
- ΔP is the change in the bond's price.
- Δy is the change in yield (typically one basis point, i.e., 0.01%).

Looking at the table, this trader has a DV01 exposure in the month of February of −$139. This means that for every 0.01 percent increase in February interest rates, the trader would lose $139 across the February cashflows of all parks and loans combined. The trader would want to flatten (that is, eliminate) this DV01 exposure and bring it down to zero in order to be immunized from interest rate risk. If DV01 = zero, then the trader has hedged his interest rate risk; that is, they are not affected by fluctuating rates. The trader would hedge their interest rate exposure by calling the interest rate desk of a bank and letting them know they would like to hedge their rates exposure. The interest rate trader at the bank will know exactly what DV01 means and will quote the gas trader a price to hedge this risk.

The same table above shows this trader's DV01 in March is +$178. This means that for every 0.01 percent increase in March interest rates, this trader makes an incremental profit of $178 on the March cashflows of all parks and loans combined. Just because the DV01 is showing a gain today doesn't mean the trader should be happy. These rates fluctuate throughout the day. Also, the DV01 in February should not be netted out against the DV01 in March. They are apples and oranges. That would be like buying one nat gas futures month and selling a different nat gas futures month and calling yourself hedged. That is not a hedge!

In conclusion, mastering park or loan transactions requires understanding the time value of money as well as the dynamics of lending and borrowing, ensuring both profitability and strategic advantage in the energy market.

Ten for Ten: Ten Trading Strategies to Make You $10 Million per Year

In 2020, Tim, once a small-time trader, implemented two of the ten strategies listed here. Skeptical but desperate for change, he meticulously studied and applied both strategies. His first breakthrough came within months, turning modest profits into substantial gains. By year's end, Tim's disciplined application of the strategies propelled him into the ranks of millionaire traders. His story spread within the industry, inspiring others. Tim's journey from obscurity to a $10 million annual income highlighted the transformative power of strategic trading. The highest annual trading profit reported by the best performing natural gas trader interviewed during the making of this book was $1.6 billion!

Trader salaries are typically much higher than scheduler salaries. Most traders are risk-takers and also have less job security if their risk-taking results in large losses for their companies. Higher risk translates to higher rewards. Trader roles are highly sought after. Typical trader salaries can range from low- to mid-six figures, not including annual bonuses. Traders also receive bonuses in terms of a percentage of profits. These percentages are variable. Large energy companies that hire speculative traders typically pay 5 to 10 percent of annual trading profits as annual bonuses. On the high end, some hedge funds pay up to 25 percent on annual trading profits. Job security is high, and benefits are plentiful at large companies. Job security is very low and benefits are almost nonexistent at hedge funds that have the highest payouts. Traders decide for themselves what type of role best suits their personality. Younger traders may be more open to taking high risks. Older traders may value job security and benefits more.

Not every scheduler aspires to be a trader. But for those who do, I have listed some concrete steps you can take to make this transition easier. Most companies will place a dollar value on each trader's seat. Here is one example of how one actual energy trading shop determines the annual bonus of a natural gas trader with eight years of experience:

> Annual gross profit generated from trading: +$25,000,000
>
> Trader annual base salary: -$250,000
>
> Trader annual benefits package (health, dental, vision, and so on): -$18,000
>
> Annual cost of seat (Bloomberg terminal, ICE account, research subscriptions, scheduler salaries, and so on): -$3,000,000
>
> Annual net profit generated from trading: $21,72,3000
>
> **Trader's annual bonus (15 percent guaranteed per contract): $3,259,800**

As you can see, the break-even cost of this trader's seat is $3,268,000 per year ($3M + $250k + $18k). A trader must generate at least this much in profit to get paid a zero bonus. Traders who lose a significant amount in any given year may get fired, especially if they have no track record of generating profits. The bonus paid each year is independent of the prior year's bonus. Some companies may even tie a portion of a trader's bonus to the group performance. This incentivizes traders to help one another out by sharing information, thereby driving up the firm's profit. However, many traders do not like the idea of a shared profit pool. Traders who believe they can achieve outsized profits individually would prefer to keep 100 percent of their spoils rather than share it with other traders whom they believe to be average or underperformers. It is up to the head of trading in every shop to determine whether profits will be reported as a pool or whether each trader's profit will be tracked individually. Most utilities and energy companies prefer the former approach. Almost every hedge fund will choose the latter.

Here are the top ten real-world actual trading strategies employed by natural gas traders in the U.S. market from 2008 to 2024 that yielded the highest absolute profits in dollar terms. These strategies are explained by several natural gas traders who were interviewed during the making of this book.

Strategy 1: Stockpile for a Rainy Day

Annual profit target: $2 million to $15 million

The highest storage trading annual profit reported by the best performing trader interviewed during the making of this book was $1.2 billion.

Having gas in a storage tank is like having money in the bank. You will always have the molecules, and that gives you flexibility to sell when prices are high. Storage space can be leased from pipelines, and gas can be stored when prices are low and sold when prices are high. We know that due to regulatory pressure in these times, not many new pipelines are receiving approval for construction. If they are, they are being delayed by environmentalists who oppose fossil fuels like natural gas. With too much shale gas and not enough pipelines, storage space becomes necessary. Storage acts like a sponge to absorb excess gas when it is not needed and release gas when it is most needed. In order to have even more flexibility, buy storage space on those pipes that are well connected with multiple natural gas pipelines. This gives you a bigger market (more liquidity) for buying and selling gas.

Most storage traders are looking at the spread between where physical gas prices (cash) is trading relative to some futures contract (usually the front month futures contract). When the spread is wide due to cash being weak (that is, cash price < futures price), traders will inject gas into storage. When the spread is wide due to cash being strong (that is, cash price > futures price), traders will withdraw gas from storage. As long as traders can cover the injection and withdrawal costs, they will keep repeating this activity, thereby locking in profits each time they inject or withdraw. If the spread is not wide enough between the cash price and the futures price, it means the traders can neither inject nor withdraw. They are not able to cover their injection and withdrawal costs. Hence, they do nothing. However, even doing nothing has a cost.

Traders bleed reservation cost (sunk cost), which we discussed in the chapter on storage valuation. They still have to pay the pipeline a sunk cost just for having reserved space (similar to having a reserved seat on an airplane). In option trading terms, this is referred to as bleeding "theta." *Theta* is the Greek letter that represents time. Everything in life has an opportunity cost. If you're doing one thing, it means you're automatically not doing another. This is the risk involved in this strategy. If the spread between cash prices and futures prices stays narrow, the traders will lose money. Each morning when I walked into my job at JPMorgan, I was down just due to bleeding theta overnight. Theta is the rent you pay in order to have a shot at making a profit each day. As Milton Friedman says, "There is no free lunch in trading." But this should not deter a trader. After all, in any strategy, the only way to make money is if prices move (that is, there is volatility). And natural gas is one of the most volatile commodities one can trade.

From this perspective, a trader should not worry about bleeding theta. A trader gets paid to take risk. Storage trading involves being able to inject gas opportunistically when prices are low and withdraw gas opportunistically when prices are high. During the peak days of the summer or winter, cash prices can diverge significantly from futures prices, albeit for a very short period of time. This is why traders stay glued to their screens and even eat lunch at their desks. Since the opportunity to make the most money in commodity markets happens only on a few days during the entire year, traders must stay vigilant all year round. This is like a surfer waiting for the perfect wave. Sure, they catch small waves every day. But the Big Kahuna comes only once a year, maybe! You don't want to miss that.

Let's assume a trader rents 1 Bcf of storage space for one year. Let's assume this is a high-turn storage facility like Egan Storage. We discussed the concept of high-turn storage, in which the trader can fill up and empty the storage space multiple times. It's like filling up a water bottle and then emptying it completely, repeating the same strategy until your one-year lease runs out. During normal times, storage traders can make a $0.05 profit per MMBtu on injections and withdrawals. During extreme scenarios, storage traders can make profits anywhere from $0.25 to hundreds of dollars per MMBtu.

Let's assume that this trader fills up his 1 Bcf of storage space with gas before the winter starts. Let's assume this trader experiences a polar vortex, which causes gas (cash) prices to shoot up $30/MMBtu above the futures price for five days in the entire winter season. In this case, the trader will max-withdraw and sell the gas from storage and buy back the futures contract, thereby locking in a $25/MMBtu profit after paying withdrawal costs (of, say, $5/MMBtu) to the pipeline. Let's assume they were able to withdraw half the gas in their storage (0.5 Bcf or 500,000 MMBtus). Their approximate profit would be $12,500,000 ($25 profit × 100,000 MMBtus × 5 days). As you can see, just this one strategy alone could result in a significant profit depending on the number of cold days in the winter and how extreme the price moves are on those days.

Strategy 2: Find PALs

Annual profit target: $1 million to $3 million

By PALs, I mean park or loan transactions. The rationale and mechanics for PAL transactions were discussed in detail in the chapter on park and loan transactions earlier in this book. PALs are deals any trader in the market can execute. The volume and profit for a PAL transaction can vary from pipe to pipe. Volumes for PALs can vary anywhere from 10,000 to 1 million MMBtus. The trader's profit share can vary anywhere from $0.05 to $1.75 per MMBtu. Let's assume a small PAL trade with a volume of 150,000 MMBtus with a profit of $0.20/MMBtu. In this case, the trader's profit is $30,000 (150,000 × $0.20). For a large-size PAL transaction, a trader's profit could be $100,000. Depending on each trader's risk appetite, traders can execute enough PALs to book profits ranging from $1 million to $3 million per year.

This is a valuable strategy to implement. Think of PALs as one of the tools in your Swiss Army Knife. PALs are required by the Federal Energy Regulatory Commission (FERC) mandate to be reported publicly on every pipeline's website (on their EBB, or electronic bulletin board) under the section "Transactional Reporting." Anyone can go and view the park and loan transactions that were done in the market by any trader with any pipeline. However, most pipelines will remove this data from their website after 90 days. Then it's gone forever! This was always a complaint of many gas traders, including myself, because this was valuable data that was lost.

But worry not! To solve this pain point, I created the gas transactional reporting (gTRAN) software. Now you can find all historical PALs that have disappeared from the pipeline EBBs. You can even use AI to quickly query these deals. You'll be able to look up the historical revenue share (profit) paid by each trader to each pipeline for every PAL transaction. Other details like receipt and delivery location, tenor, rate schedule, and more are also included. This software can be found here:

https://www.NatGasHub.com/gTRAN

Strategy 3: Cherry-Pick Capacity Releases

Annual profit target: $500,000 to $1 million

There is a secondary market for trading and exchanging unused storage space and transport space on many pipelines. One person's trash is another's treasure. If you're not participating in the capacity release market, you may be overlooking valuable opportunities to enhance your trading profits. Nat gas traders I interviewed have stated they can expect to make an average of $500,000 to $1 million dollars per year by scooping up capacity at a discount from another shipper who does not have a need for their capacity. This happens due to many reasons. For instance, a utility that owns firm storage or firm transport may not have any demand during a certain time period. They may want to release (resell) all or a portion of their capacity to another trader. This is like subleasing your apartment for rent when you're away. I have personally experienced this pain point when trying to search for biddable capacity. When I was trading nat gas, there was not any real time, user-friendly, reliable way to identify these opportunities. The only way to do this was to stare at every pipeline's website and hope someone posts a bid or an offer that might be attractive. It was like watching paint dry. Neither I nor my schedulers had the time to stare at still water and hope to catch some fish. In the trading world, hope is the worst strategy. It was for this specific purpose that I created an automated service using AI that gathers data, standardizes it, and alerts a trader in real time as to when the money tree is ready to be shaken.

There are certain types of capacity releases that could be lucrative. This type of release is called an asset management agreement (AMA). An AMA is a specialized contractual arrangement in which a capacity holder, known as the releasing shipper, transfers its transportation capacity on a pipeline or gas supply management to an asset manager. This asset manager, often a third-party entity or a marketing affiliate, takes on the responsibility of managing these resources to optimize their use, typically aiming to minimize costs and maximize efficiency and profitability. AMAs generally involve the following components:

Capacity release: The releasing shipper grants the asset manager rights to its pipeline transportation capacity. This can include firm transportation rights, which guarantee the asset manager priority access to pipeline space.

Supply management: The asset manager oversees the procurement, scheduling, and delivery of natural gas supplies. This includes balancing the supply and demand to meet the releasing shipper's needs while taking advantage of market opportunities.

Fee structure: Compensation for the asset manager is typically performance-based, involving a fee or a share of the savings and profits generated through optimized management. This incentivizes the asset manager to achieve the best possible outcomes.

Regulatory compliance: AMAs must comply with Federal Energy Regulatory Commission (FERC) regulations, ensuring transparency and fairness in the capacity release process. This includes adhering to open-access requirements and nondiscriminatory practices.

AMAs benefit releasing shippers by allowing them to leverage the expertise and market knowledge of asset managers, leading to more efficient use of pipeline capacity and gas supplies, cost savings, and enhanced operational flexibility. For asset managers, these agreements provide an opportunity to utilize their expertise in trading, logistics, and market analysis to generate profits.

Cherry-pick capacity release deals here in one place that you won't find anywhere else:

https://www.NatGasHub.com/Capacity

Strategy 4: Establish Beachheads

Annual profit target: $1 million to $1.5 million

When your car breaks down in Houston, a tow truck from Dallas is not going to rescue you. You will have to call a local towing company in Houston. Look out for when things break in the gas market. We know it is getting harder and harder to build new pipes. Hence, the infrastructure growth is limited. Yon can only flow so much gas through a pipe. This strategy looks for those opportunities when economics and physics are at odds with each other. From a pure engineering (physics) perspective, there may be only so much space available on a pipeline to carry gas. When the pipeline shuts down unexpectedly, that gas has nowhere to go. Flaring (burning unwanted natural gas) laws are becoming more stringent with stiff penalties. This means producers must sell gas at negative prices just to get rid of it. This scenario played out in April 2024 when the El Paso pipeline shut down unexpectedly, causing Waha prices to go negative. I call this the "thy cup runneth over" strategy. What made this problem worse is that the same producers who were producing natural gas were also producing oil. The oil was far more profitable than the natural gas, so much so that Waha prices would have to go $7.00 negative before the producers would stop producing natural gas. Another way to think about this is that the burgers were selling for such a high price that the owner didn't care if they gave away the fries for free.

The most successful strategy in this case would have been to establish a year-round "beachhead" at Waha. This means that you pick certain regions (for example, Waha) and become an expert in those areas. You figure out a way to move the unwanted gas by injecting it into storage or finding a way to get the gas to a buyer who needs it. You become one of the only few tow truck drivers available. You may sit idle for some time. But when stranded drivers need you, you can charge enough of a premium to pay for all the idle time. An astute physical natural gas trader will pick an area that is prone to such irregular shortages. Once you establish a beachhead at Waha, move to the neighboring suburb and establish another beachhead there. This way, a trader can expand their business empire, their trading profits, and their personal compensation.

The most successful traders are those who are patient. In the long run, every trader is right. But you don't have an eternity to sit on your trading position. Every trader has a time limit and a risk limit. The more patience a trader can exhibit, the more chances they have to turn a profit on their trade. All markets are cyclical, and natural gas is no exception. Your position may turn negative before it turns positive. The question is, will your boss panic or allow you to keep your position long enough to allow your conviction to play out? In my experience, and after interviewing several traders, the conclusion is that most times a trader will be forced to liquidate their position because their boss did not want to take additional risk.

If you have all the data about how much the producers are producing and how much the consumers need, you need to estimate at what time of the year these two forces will collide. That will cause prices to dislocate.

Strategy 5: Buy Lottery Tickets

Annual profit target: $3.5 million

The highest transport trading annual profit reported by the best performing trader interviewed during the making of this book was $1.6 billion. For this strategy, a trader would acquire pipeline transport space into congested areas with extreme weather. Two popular routes or pipelines on which to acquire transport are (1) NGPL Pipeline into Chicago, and (2) Algonquin, Iroquois, TETCO, or Transco Pipeline into the New York City area. As one veteran gas trader said to me, "Not many traders make it into the 'Nat Gas Hall of Fame' being short New York City gas in the winter"! If you own transport into Chicago or New York City in the winter months (November through March) and it turns out to be a real cold winter for a prolonged period of time, you will print money! If last winter was warm, chances are, next winter may not be. If you've had two or three warm winters in a row, that should give you even more confidence that the next winter may be colder than normal. Play the probabilities. There is more weather data available than there is stock market data. What is the probability of having two winters back-to-back in New York City that are warmer than usual? What about three winters or four winters? Do the same analysis for Chicago. It doesn't have to stay cold for all 151 days in winter from November 1 to March 31. Or if it's a leap year, then 152 days. Hey, every extra day increases the probability of you winning the lottery! Extreme cold weather for even five or ten days in the winter can make you a couple million dollars on a volume of 10,000 to 20,000 MMBtus/day.

Here's how the math works. When extreme cold hits Chicago or New York City, gas cash prices could be trading anywhere from $20 to $50 per MMBtu above normal. Let's assume a modest scenario where there is a polar blast in New York City spanning five days in which cash prices trade $35 above normal for five days. You own 20,000 MMBtus per day of firm transport. A back-of-the-envelope calculation will tell you this would result in a profit of approximately $3,500,000 ($35/MMBtu × 20,000 MMBtus/day × 5 days). During winter storm Yuri in Texas in 2021, cash prices were trading in some areas at $900 to $1,000 per MMBtu above normal! Not bad for a lottery ticket that worked five days in the whole year!

As market prices fluctuate, the pipeline tariff stays the same. In other words, as prices go higher, your costs stay the same. The rationale behind buying lottery tickets in the nat gas market is that most money is made in very small periods of time, where prices move to extreme levels but revert back to normal very quickly. A trader's entire year's profit target could be made on ten or fifteen days in the year. If they are lucky, these ten days occur at the beginning of the year. That way, they have achieved their annual profit target and locked in their annual bonus as early as February. They do not need to take a whole lot of risk for the rest of the year. They could be sipping Mai Tais in Costa Rica for most of that year. In fact, that is exactly what one trader did, whom I interviewed for the making of this book!

Keep in mind that you don't have to buy the actual pipeline transport to play in this market. You could just trade the financial (paper) basis. That is a riskier strategy, but it is easier and cheaper to execute. Buying transport involves paying a sunk cost (reservation charge) to the pipeline. You also have to buy physical gas molecules and make sure they flow on the pipe during the coldest days of the year. If you trade paper basis, you do not have to worry about buying and selling physical gas and also do not have to submit any pipeline nominations. Buying lottery tickets is a proven strategy, not just in the nat gas market but also in other markets like oil, electricity, stocks, and bonds.

Strategy 6: Use Automation to Increase Revenue

Annual profit target: $1 million to $3 million

Traders must spend a lot of time researching the market to give themselves an information edge. I could present the same news article to two different traders, and one would reach a buy decision while the other would be a seller. The quality and timeliness of data is very important to trading decisions. After all, time is money! Free up the time of your traders and schedulers who are doing manual data scraping across over 100 different pipeline websites, hand-typing nominations, manually monitoring and updating pipeline tariffs, and so many more error-prone mundane tasks that take away precious time from your traders and schedulers. These people are your revenue generators. If you have a salesperson working at Coca-Cola, their entire job must entail sales every minute of the day. If they are doing administrative jobs, that takes away precious time. Coca-Cola would not be able to meet its annual profit target if its salespeople were hamstrung by being forced to perform manual tasks not related to sales. In the gas industry, as an example, the old-fashioned way of submitting noms to pipelines has evolved over time from faxed noms to hand-typed noms to electronic EDI noms. If you're still hand-typing noms the old-fashioned way, your company may be heading into extinction.

Traders and schedulers must petition their business leaders to automate their manual tasks, thereby making them mean, lean revenue machines! Automation also leads to less stress, higher skill level, and happier, more satisfied employees. Companies like Amazon and Apple have become trillion-dollar companies because they offer one-click nirvana. Amazon experienced an increase in sales by implementing the one-click buy button on their website. If you give your employees the gift of free time, they will give you the gift of increased profits.

If you are a trading shop, the way to grow your revenue is to run more volume through your trading factory. You want to be able to do more trades with the same number of people. But your people have only a limited number of hours each day. Technology is the tool that helps you scale your business. ICE (Intercontinental Exchange), the largest exchange for trading natural gas today, started as a very niche software built by Enron traders in the early 1990s. It was originally called Enron Online. Today, ICE owns the New York Stock Exchange, among many other exchanges around the world. ICE realized that the only way to explode their revenue was to run more trades through its software without exploding headcount. ICE is basically a technology company. Once its software was able to do what traders needed it to do, the next thing was adding more trade volume, more users, and running it through the same software.

This tilt in your strategy toward technology and automation could be the game-changing shot-in-the-arm your trading organization needs to explode your profits. This technological advancement would also help you acquire with confidence your struggling competitors. There have been many such recent acquisitions of trading books of struggling companies by competitors, and these will only accelerate with better technology. For example, JPMorgan acquires Bear Stearns's and Sempra's nat gas trading books, Mercuria acquires JPMorgan's nat gas trading book, Williams acquires Sequent's nat gas trading book, Macquarie acquires Cargill's nat gas trading book, Citi acquires K2 Commodities's nat gas trading book, and many more.

Having worked personally on the JPMorgan acquisitions, as an example, the strategy behind acquiring these trade books of struggling competitors is to haircut the value of their nat gas trades, reduce headcount, and book a large day-one gain upon closing the deal. The JPMorgan acquisition of Sempra resulted in JPMorgan being awarded the accolade of "Natural Gas House of the Year" by *Energy Risk* magazine in 2012.

These transactions would not have been possible without the acquirers having the proper technology in-house to digest competitor trade books.

Let's look at it from a numbers perspective. Let's say you have one trader whose annual profit target is $10 million. They have 2,000 working hours in a year to hit this $10 million target. A trader spends anywhere from 20 percent to 40 percent of their daily time reading research reports, manually booking trades, updating spreadsheets, monitoring multiple different pipeline websites, reading pipeline critical notices, running profit or loss reports, correcting data entry errors, and other administrative tasks. These are all tasks in which technology can drastically reduce the amount of time spent. For example, one basic task traders do every day is read research reports to arrive at a buy or sell decision. They may be reading research reports published by two different analysts and reading a weather report published by one analyst. But what if they could use a software that automatically reads the research reports published by all twelve analysts and all five meteorologists in the market and gives them a buy or sell recommendation? This software is a Language Learning Model (LLM) that is the brain of every AI software. Because it's an LLM, it can read and understand what another human wrote. It can read the research reports of all twelve analysts and provide a bullish or bearish sentiment, all within a few minutes!

Another frequent complaint of traders is that they have to read every pipeline critical notice. These notices could be issued at any time and must be monitored via email. Traders already receive hundreds of emails every day. Most traders confess they do not have time to read all the critical notices, especially the ones that contain market-moving information. This is another area where AI software can help by reading every incoming pipeline notice automatically and only alerting the trader to read the ones that contain market moving information. This way, a trader can tune out the noise and focus on revenue generation. To eliminate this specific pain point, I built the gNOTICE product infused with AI capability to automatically help nat gas traders. It is a tool that I wish had been available when I was trading. More information can be found here:

https://www.NatGasHub.com/Products

    Another pain point in the gas business that results in countless wasted hours is schedulers having to do nomination triple entry. One time they will enter their gas noms into their spreadsheets. The second time they will hand-type the same noms into every pipeline website. The third time, they will have to input those same noms into their in-house ETRM system. By eliminating triple-entry and freeing up the time of schedulers, you are allowing them to work on more revenue generating opportunities, for example, expanding your business footprint to new pipes, spotting cash trading opportunities, avoiding pipeline imbalance penalties, tracking pipeline open seasons, monitoring pipeline notices, scouring the market for capacity releases, and so much more.

    Even more hours are spent monitoring pipeline tariff changes, scraping them manually from various pipeline websites, and hand-typing these tariff changes into your ETRM system. This entire pain point of updating tariffs manually every day can now be eliminated by the gTARIFF product, which I created to help schedulers. More information can be found here: https://www.NatGasHub.com/Products. Automating these manual tasks could free up 25 percent to 50 percent of your scheduler's daily time, thereby allowing them to focus on revenue generation while increasing their skill level and job satisfaction.

Strategy 7: Algorithmic Trading

Annual Profit Target: $500k

In some natural gas products, like the front month on the NYMEX futures contract, machines have already taken over a substantial portion of the daily trading activity. Algorithmic trading works by using computer programs to execute trades automatically based on predefined criteria, such as price, volume, or timing, without the need for human intervention. Momentum trading algorithms are discussed here that have been employed successfully by natural gas traders to reap profits.

Momentum trading algos are designed to pinpoint a pronounced trend in one direction and take advantage of the trend's persistence, no matter how the trend arises. For example, when meteorologists release their updated daily short-term weather predictions, the natural gas futures prices may start moving either up or down. This fluctuation is short-lived. However, traders can exploit this price movement. Once new information (for example, a weather forecast) is released, a computer algo can detect (faster than a human) in which direction the prices have started trending (up or down). This is similar to an expert surfer jumping on to the surfboard right before a new wave picks up. Once they catch the wave, they can ride it out for a few seconds. Those few seconds are enough for an algo strategy to make lightning fast buy and sell decisions to lock in profits.

This kind of strategy has a few requirements: There must be a market event (like weather updates) that happens at a set time every day. An expert software developer would need to build an algo (with a trader's help) that automatically executes buy or sell decisions. The algo would start operating when it detects (1) a price "wave" has started, and (2) in which direction (price up or down) a wave is moving. The first few price ticks are crucial in making this decision within microseconds. The algo would make quick buy and sell decisions repeatedly.

Let's say the algo detects that the price has started trending upward. The algo would buy low and sell high to lock in the first profit. It would then buy higher and sell even higher to lock in the second profit. This way, it would repeat these buy-sell loops as the price wave keeps rising. The algo would also need to know the transaction cost charged by the exchange for each buy or sell trade. The algo trading strategy must be profitable after paying for all transaction costs. Algo traders will typically make $2,000 to $5,000 for a price movement spanning around ten seconds. Only a computer could make decisions this fast. The algo would then monitor when the price "wave" is slowing down. At that point, the algo would automatically stop trading. Such an algo would not trade every time the price moves. It would only trade when a specific event occurs, such as a change in the weather forecast. Using this strategy, traders can build algos for multiple events that occur at predictable times during the trading day. Using a conservative approach, let's say a trader could make $3,500 per day. Let's assume the algo runs for only 150 out of the 252 trading days in the year. This trader would have locked in an annual profit of $525,000 ($3,500/day × 150 days). The most popular programming language for algorithmic trading is Python.

Pros of algo trading: Algorithms execute trades quickly and efficiently, without emotional bias, leading to potentially higher returns and reduced transaction costs.

Cons of algo trading: Algorithmic trading strategies can be complex and require significant technical expertise, and there's a risk of unexpected market behavior leading to losses.

Algorithmic trading requires a careful balance, in which the advantages of speed and efficiency are weighed against the need for cautious risk management and oversight, making it essential to develop a robust algo trading strategy.

Strategy 8: Find Deep-Pocketed Clients

Annual profit target: $1 million

Microsoft, Google, Amazon, Meta, and so many other tech companies are embarking on a massive data center buildout.

> *"The world adds a new data center every three days."*
> — **Bill Vass**, VP of Engineering, Amazon Web Services

The nat gas industry has a new deep-pocketed client: the AI industry! The nat gas industry is poised to become a key supplier to the AI industry for its insatiable energy needs. Data centers need electricity 24/7 to house cloud applications, run AI models, and run air conditioners to cool their servers. Data centers needed to advance AI will require so much energy they could strain the power grid and stymie the transition to cleaner energy sources. "Utilities will have to lean more heavily on natural gas, coal, and nuclear plants," said former U.S. Energy Secretary Ernest Moniz. Big Tech is not going to wait ten years to get new solar or wind infrastructure built. That leaves you with natural gas, which already has infrastructure built, is cheap, is reliable 24/7, and has a lower carbon footprint than coal. The new partnership between AI and the nat gas industry is a win-win.

Traders who want to capitalize on this new source of demand can sell gas directly to data centers. If you can't sell to data centers directly, then sell indirectly through utilities. All the utilities are ramping up their demand projections due to data centers. Traders should acquire more utility, municipal, and retail energy customers into your portfolio. Estimates for new demand created by data centers range from 2 Bcf per day to 20 Bcf per day.

Let's assume a conservative scenario of 5 Bcf per day incremental demand from new data centers being built over the next ten years. Let's assume you can sell nat gas to data center clients to the tune of 100,000 MMBtus per day for one year (365 days) and make a modest profit of $0.03 per MMBtu. A back-of-the-envelope calculation of annual profit on this new incremental demand would be $1,095,000 ($0.03/MMBtu profit × 100,000 MMBtus/day × 365 days). Every country is in the midst of data center buildouts. "It's a very hungry caterpillar," said Yukio Kani, CEO, JERA, Japan. Japan is also embarking on building out data centers. As a trader, your job is to find the caterpillar, feed it, and get rewarded handsomely!

Strategy 9: Money Saved Is Money Earned

Annual profit target: $1 million

Minimize trading costs by getting open credit from counterparties. When a counterparty does not give you credit, you must post a letter of credit (LC) to trade with them. This is referred to as posting collateral. Even if they do give you credit, if you exceed the credit limit, you must post collateral to your counterparties. This is very similar to how your credit card works. Most traders I know do not know or care to know about credit costs because in most companies, credit costs are not billed against a trader's profit or loss. But these are real costs. Your trading organization as a whole pays for this.

There are tricks to minimizing or even eliminating these costs. Every cost eliminated is an increase in your company's annual trading profit. LC costs typically range from $0.01 to $0.05 of the value of the LC. For instance, if your company's LC cost is $0.01 per $1 million in the value of the LC, then your LC costs is $10,000 ($0.01 × $1,000,000). This is what it costs your company to buy $1 million worth of gas from someone who gives you zero credit. This is the same as shopping at Walmart with a credit card that has a zero credit limit. You must pay interest to the bank to use this credit card for any purchases you make. In the banking industry, this is referred to as secured credit: for every $1 in credit you receive, you must have $1 in your bank account to back it up. You can obtain your company's LC cost from your treasurer or CFO.

If your LC cost is $0.01 and you would like to save $1 million per year in LC costs, then you would need to obtain $100 million in open credit from all your trading counterparties combined. Open credit means that a counterparty will sell you gas without any collateral because your company's credit rating is high enough that the counterparty is not worried about you going bankrupt in the next 60 days. Your credit risk manager knows exactly who gives you how much credit. They know this because each time you exceed a counterparty's credit risk, your credit manager's phone will start ringing. It will keep ringing until you pay up the collateral they demand.

The best way to increase your company's credit rating (which is like a person's FICO score) is to reduce your debt and make your company's balance sheet look sexy. But that is not always an easy task. Another way to do this is through relationship building. Have your company's credit manager attend the International Energy Credit Association (IECA) conference every year. There are other conferences they can attend too. Tie your credit manager's annual performance bonus to how much open credit they can secure for your company. Treat your credit manager like a trader and evaluate them on hard criteria, just like you evaluate a trader based on hard numbers like profit or loss. That is the low-hanging fruit. Start there.

You may also see a lot of red on ICE. Seeing red in trader lingo means that you can't get matched up with counterparties on ICE because you don't have a trading relationship with them or because they give you zero credit. If a counterparty gives you zero credit, meaning they think that you are a risky customer (a bank criteria for which they will deny you a loan), then you will have to find another counterparty who may sell you gas at a higher price. This is a double whammy. Not only are you losing money (because you have to post cash collateral), but you also have to pay a higher price to buy gas from another counterparty.

Here's another strategy employed by smart trading shops. You can also create credit for yourself. How? Before the start of the month, you can sell a bunch of index gas to a counterparty who gives you zero credit. Selling index-priced gas is very low risk. You can do a back-to-back deal in which you buy index from one counterparty and sell index-priced gas to another counterparty for zero profit. Let's assume that Counterparty A is a very large bank, but they give you zero credit because they think you are a default risk. You would really like to buy gas from Counterparty A, but you can't due to credit restrictions. Let's say Counterparty B gives you a $5 million open line of credit. What you would do is buy $5 million worth of gas at an IFERC index price for delivery next month from Counterparty B without having to post any collateral. This is like an interest-free loan. Then you would turn around and sell $5 million worth of IFERC index-price gas to Counterparty A at that location or any other liquid location. You bought IFERC Index at one location. You sold IFERC index at another location. By doing so, you effectively turned Counterparty A (a large bank) into someone who now owes you money.

Most trading contracts have netting provision. This means that all the buys and sells with a specific counterparty at all locations are netted against one another for that specific counterparty. For each counterparty, your credit risk manager has a net exposure (that is, you are either a net buyer or a net seller to each counterparty). Your goal is to be a net seller (by selling index-priced gas) to those counterparties who give you zero credit. Be a net buyer (by buying index-prices gas) from those counterparties that give you open unsecured credit. This is like maximizing your credit card limit each month but not going over. If you pay your credit card bill each month, you get charged zero interest from the bank. It's the same concept in gas trading.

To simplify this idea, consider a scenario: Let's say every month you only buy gas from one counterparty, and you only sell gas to one other counterparty. Your seller gives you $5 million of open credit, and you buy $5 million of gas from them. You don't have to post any LC. Your credit cost is zero. Then you turn around and sell $5 million worth of gas to the other counterparty for a profit of $0.01 per MMBtu. In this simplistic scenario, your credit cost is zero. Your trading profit is $0.01. Rinse and repeat the same strategy, and you'll be booking profits each month.

In the gas industry, a shipper pays for gas every month. By selling gas to a counterparty first, you are essentially opening up the ability for all the other traders in your shop to buy back gas from that same counterparty at any pipeline location. Without these offsetting credit trades, you would not be able to trade with certain counterparties. Another strategy you can use is to clear the physical gas trades through an exchange like ICE Natural Gas Exchange (NGX). NGX is a division of ICE that steps in between you and the counterparty when there is a credit restriction. NGX charges a fee for this service. Both counterparties now face NGX instead of each other. Since NGX is backed by the faith and credit of ICE, each counterparty is comfortable being in this trade. It's a win-win-win for all three entities involved.

Strategy 10: Weather-Contingent Natural Gas Options

Annual profit target: $500k/year

As global warming picks up, many cities are likely to experience extreme weather events that are short-lived. Utilities operating in various cities across the U.S. need to buy natural gas every day of the year. Inclement weather could hit their earnings at any time. Most utilities do not have weather insurance but would like to have this protection. Many utilities across the country have approval from their public utility commissions to charge their ratepayers for this insurance. Utilities hold auctions every year in which they put out requests for proposals (RFPs) to buy weather-contingent natural gas options. There is more weather data than there is stock market data, but selling options is a risky strategy—especially selling naked call options. If you do implement this strategy, ensure you have a way to obtain gas on cold days when a utility is likely to call for the gas.

A weather-contingent natural gas option is a financial derivative that combines elements of weather derivatives and natural gas options. These instruments are designed to hedge or speculate on the impact of weather conditions on natural gas prices or consumption. Here's a detailed breakdown of what a weather-contingent natural gas option entails:

Key features:

- Underlying asset:
  - The underlying asset for this option is natural gas.
- Weather variable:
  - The option is contingent on specific weather conditions, such as temperature, degree days (heating degree days or cooling degree days), or other weather-related metrics. The most common weather variables used are temperature and degree days.
- Trigger conditions:
  - The payout of the option is triggered based on the occurrence of predefined weather conditions. For example, a heating degree day (HDD)-contingent option might pay out if the number of HDDs exceeds a certain threshold, indicating colder-than-expected weather, which typically increases natural gas demand for heating.

How it works:

- Hedging against weather risk:
  - Natural gas consumers or producers can use these options to hedge against the financial risk associated with adverse weather conditions. For instance, a natural gas utility might purchase a weather-contingent option to protect against a colder-than-expected winter, which could increase heating demand and, consequently, decrease their revenue (since they would have to buy expensive gas in the spot market). Their revenue is capped by regulators (state public utility commissions). They can only charge preapproved rates to residential and commercial consumers.
- Structure of the option:
  - The option specifies a strike price, which is the price level at which the option can be exercised. In this case, the strike price is the temperature in a given city.
  - The payout depends on the natural gas price and the weather variable. For example, if the temperature at Houston Hobby Airport for a certain date falls below 32 degrees Fahrenheit, then the utility has the right to buy natural gas at a preset price, no matter where the price is trading in the market.
- Pricing:
  - The pricing of these options involves complex modeling, combining natural gas market volatility with weather forecasts and historical weather data. The premium for the option will depend on the likelihood of the specified weather conditions occurring.

Example:

Consider a natural gas utility, like CenterPoint Energy, serving the Houston, Texas, metropolis that wants to hedge against the risk of a cold winter (lower cooling degree days [CDDs]). They could purchase a weather-contingent natural gas option with the following terms:

- **Daily strike price:** 32 degrees Fahrenheit for temperature; $3.50/MMBtu for the price of gas at the Houston Ship Channel (HSC) location traded on ICE
- **Volume:** 10,000 MMBtus/day
- **Weather station:** Houston Hobby Airport
- **Profit/loss:** (Market price − strike price) × Volume
- **Term:** November 1, 2024, through March 31, 2025

If the actual temperature at Houston Hobby Airport settles at 30 degrees Fahrenheit for a given flow date, then CenterPoint would have the right to buy the gas at $3.50, no matter what the price is trading on ICE. Let's say that on ICE, the price of gas being traded for tomorrow's flow date at the HSC Location is $4.00/MMBtu. The payout would be as follows:

Profit/loss calculation = (market price − strike price) × volume

= ($4.00 − $3.50) × 10,000

= $5,000

This profit/loss calculation reflects the loss avoided by CenterPoint by not having to pay higher prices to buy gas on ICE. The option seller would lose $5,000 for having to buy expensive gas on ICE and selling it cheaper to CenterPoint.

Benefits:

- Risk management:
  - Provides a way for natural gas market participants to manage the risk associated with weather variability, which can significantly impact natural gas consumption and prices.
- Customizable:
  - These options can be tailored to meet specific needs, including different weather variables, thresholds, and payout structures.
- Market efficiency:
  - Enhances market efficiency by allowing more precise hedging of weather-related risks, leading to better price discovery and stability in natural gas markets.

Weather-contingent natural gas options are innovative financial instruments that help market participants manage the financial risks associated with weather fluctuations. By linking weather conditions with natural gas prices, these options provide a valuable tool for hedging and risk management in the energy sector.

Bonus Strategy 11: Don't Be Stranded on an Island

Annual profit target: $2.5 million to $3 million

Prior to the U.S. liquified natural gas (LNG) market opening up for exports, the U.S. natural gas market was an island. There was no way to get U.S.-produced natural gas out into the other parts of the world. Cheniere built the first export terminal. That was the first bridge connecting the U.S. island to the rest of the world. Now many new LNG terminals are built or are in the works: in other words, many new "bridges" are being built. LNG is your release valve. If you want to tap into international markets, acquire LNG customers.

Some U.S.-based nat gas traders may want to integrate vertically by building or acquiring LNG terminals. That is another way to muscle out competitor traders and directly access the LNG market by eliminating the middleman. The main goal is to be able to sell your gas to an international clientele. The price of natural gas in the U.S. is currently the cheapest. Supply-wise, the U.S. is in a dominant position and is referred to as the Saudi Arabia of nat gas. The four top global producers of nat gas are Saudi Arabia, Russia, the United States, and Qatar. The U.S. has the most stable regime of the four and the strongest business laws of any of the top LNG producers in the world. The U.S. can also produce LNG responsibly by sourcing the gas from producers who can furnish certificates to prove a low-carbon footprint. Russian-domiciled gas producers are not credible when it comes to certifying that their LNG was produced responsibly with a low-carbon footprint.

Energy is the ultimate currency. This is because you can print currency, but you can't print oil or gas molecules. The U.S. has one of the largest proven natural gas reserves in the world. The U.S. has the molecules, and you should use this leverage to your advantage. You'd also be a hero by bringing low-carbon nat gas to the global market, which really needs it after Russian gas was shut out due to the Ukraine war.

U.S.-based nat gas traders should use these natural advantages bestowed upon the U.S. to their benefit. Look beyond U.S. shores to tap profits in places where other nat gas traders are not focusing or where they don't have the resources to reach. Let's assume you can make a modest $0.02 to $0.03 per MMBtu profit for selling 50,000 MMBtus/day of LNG for five years (1,825 days) to an international client. Here is your potential profit: $2,737,500 ($0.03 profit × 50,000 MMBtus/day × 1,825 days). The world is your oyster!

Bonus Strategy 12: Establish Your Franchise

Annual profit target: $1 million to $3 million

Singapore Airlines and Turkish Airlines both fly passengers on the same planes made by Boeing. But Singapore Airlines can command a premium price per mile flown relative to Turkish Airlines. Every Boeing airplane is the same; it's the people who make the airline different. If everyone is selling the same fungible commodity (in this case, natural gas), how do you distinguish yourself? You're flowing the same gas on the same pipeline as others. Why should someone pay you a premium? It's because you're not just selling gas. You're selling reliability. It's your reputation that will earn you a premium. When a hurricane or a winter storm hits, your clients need to know that you will be available to find them replacement gas. When your LNG client's plant trips and they are suddenly swimming in too much gas, they will pick up the phone to call someone for help. Let that someone be you. There are around 500 counterparties that are active on ICE in the natural gas physical market on any given day. Not all of them are active at every location. At some locations in the U.S., there may be just four or five counterparties who are active. Knowing your customer (KYC) will make you money!

To be a successful (and profitable) trader, build your franchise for buying and selling physical natural gas. Buying and selling physical gas profitably involves both skill and art. Your profitability from this strategy depends on how much physical gas you trade every day. Let's assume you trade 50,000 MMBtus every day. When gas prices are low, you can expect to make $0.01 to $0.05 in profit per MMBtu. When gas prices are high, you make $0.10 to $0.15 per MMBtu. In extreme cases, (like winter Storm Yuri in 2021), you could make hundreds of dollars per MMBtu. You trade with the same customers in each scenario.

Let's assume a conservative scenario in which you trade 100,000 MMBtus per day and have a good customer franchise from which you can make a profit of $0.05 per MMBtu. This translates into a profit of $5,000 per day, or $1.825 million per year. The more volume you can trade and the bigger franchise you establish, the higher your profit will be. This strategy is for those who want to take minimal risk. Most of your trades are back-to-back, meaning you have very little open risk every day. Your position is close to flat when you go home each day.

> "The most important single thing is to focus obsessively on the customer. Our goal is to be earth's most customer-centric company."
> — **Jeff Bezos**, founder, Amazon

Bonus Strategy 13: Transatlantic Riches

Annual profit target: $1 million to $3 million

Tap into Europe's gas market volatility while trading from U.S. shores. One way to take advantage of the volatility in the European gas market is to trade the Dutch title transfer facility (TTF) natural gas futures. This is Europe's equivalent of the ICE Henry Hub natural gas futures. The rationale behind this strategy is that Europe has become a big client and consumer of the U.S. natural gas via the LNG export market. In the past, both the U.S. and Russia were big suppliers of LNG into the European market. But after Russia invaded Ukraine in 2022, Russian gas supplies to Europe were curtailed, causing the TTF price to spike in August 2022 (as shown in the chart below).[2]

---

[2] Graph source: "The August 2022 Surge in the Price of Natural Gas Futures," European Securities and Markets Authority, October 24, 2023, https://www.esma.europa.eu/sites/default/files/2023-10/ESMA50-524821-2963_TRV_Article_the_August_2022_surge_in_the_price_of_natural_gas_futures.pdf (accessed June 17, 2024).

European natural gas futures prices (Dutch TTF)
Surges in February and August 2022

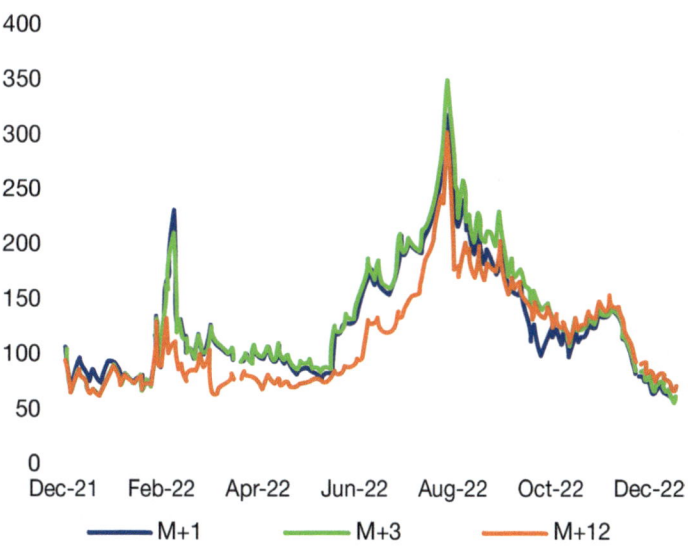

[Chart showing TTF futures prices from Dec-21 to Dec-22 for M+1, M+3, and M+12 contracts, with peaks in February 2022 (~230) and August 2022 (~350), prices ranging from about 50 to 350 EUR]

Note: Average close price observed on ICE and EEX for selected TTF Monthly contracts, in EUR.
Sources: Refinitiv EIKON, ESMA.

This price surge appears driven by strong demand among EU end-clients and the need to secure winter reserves, in the context of the fall in Russian supply. Even if the war ends, Europe may not want to go back to being dependent on gas supplies from autocratic regimes. The U.S. stands as a reliable supplier and staunch political ally of Europe for the foreseeable future. The U.S. has already become and is poised to stay as the major supplier of LNG to Europe. This makes the TTF futures price very sensitive to U.S. natural gas prices. TTF traders are watching U.S. natural gas futures very closely. U.S. traders have now started dabbling in TTF futures.

While this strategy is still new, those traders who have the risk appetite for global exposure can take advantage of this strategy. One strategy is to go outright long or short TTF futures in any given month. A less risky strategy is to put on a spread trade by going long Dutch TTF futures and short U.S. Henry Hub futures or vice versa, depending on your market view. Another strategy is to put on a spread between TTF and BalMo Henry Hub swap. The BalMo Henry Hub swap is a better proxy for the Henry Hub cash market. The reason you would want to use a cash proxy is because the TTF price movement tracks whether an LNG plant in the U.S. ramps up or down.

An LNG plant ramping up or down is going to cause movement in the BalMo cash market for physical gas. For example, if an LNG plant shuts down today due to mechanical issues, there will be too much physical gas in the spot market with nowhere to go. This will put downward pressure on the BalMo price, as traders may not know how long the outage may last. Since the LNG plant is shut down, that would cause an LNG shortage in Europe, which would cause the Dutch TTF price to spike. This volatility in the U.S. market versus the European market creates opportunities for profits.

This scenario played out in reality in the U.S. gas market. On June 8, 2022, a fire at Freeport LNG's natural gas liquefaction plant on the Gulf Coast in south Texas led to the full shutdown of the facility. The shutdown of Freeport LNG reduced total U.S. LNG export capacity by approximately 2 billion cubic feet per day (Bcf/d), or 17 percent of total U.S. LNG export capacity. This caused a 16 percent drop in the price of U.S. natural gas futures. Freeport was closed for eight months until it reopened in February 2023. TTF prices spiked to an all-time high in August 2022, as shown in the chart above. The situation was exacerbated as Russia also curtailed gas supplies (due to the Ukraine war) to Europe during the same timeframe in retaliation for economic sanctions imposed by the European Union.

Traders who intend to trade TTF futures should build their own European supply-demand model. Supply and demand data for the European market is readily available in one place on the Gas Infrastructure Europe (GIE) website: https://AGSI.GIE.EU. After you build your model, ask yourself, what is the market missing? Be humble.

I'd say, "Good luck trading!" but good traders know luck is never a strategy. As Matt Damon said in the movie *Rounders*, "People insist on calling it luck. Why do you think the same five guys make it to the final table of the World Series of Poker every year? What, are they the luckiest guys in Las Vegas? It's a skill game."

Bonus Strategy 14: Trade the News

Annual profit target: $1.5 million

In the U.S. natural gas market, there are some events that occur with regularity. Since these are publicly disclosed, traders set up positions to benefit from these preannounced events:

- EIA: One of these is the highly awaited natural gas inventory number released every Thursday morning by a government entity called the Energy Information Administration (EIA). Traders can establish long or short positions based on how much gas they believe was injected or withdrawn into or out of all storage caverns combined in the U.S. over the last seven days.
- COT: Another event occurs every Friday when a different government entity called the Commodity Futures Trading Commission (CFTC) releases the Commitment of Traders (COT) report. This report shows which category of traders are long or short natural gas futures. It gives traders an idea about which category of traders changed their view about the price of natural gas during the last seven days.
- UNG: Another event that occurs monthly is the rebalancing of the largest natural gas exchange traded fund (ETF), called the United States Natural Gas Fund LP (UNG). This ETF gives anyone in the public a chance to invest in natural gas futures indirectly by investing in the UNG. Most U.S. citizens

can't trade commercial natural gas futures contracts listed on ICE. This is because they are too risky for the average investor. The regulators also don't want thousands of people speculating directly on ICE by betting on the price of natural gas, which is a vital commodity for the U.S. economy. Hence, the only way for retail investors to gain exposure to the natural gas futures market is through ETFs like the UNG. The UNG rebalancing (or roll) occurs once a month. The date of this rebalancing is listed publicly on the UNG website. The UNG invests in futures contracts that have maturities in different months. Each month, the UNG has to sell the futures contract that is expiring and roll their money into the futures contract for another month. In effect, the UNG is selling one month and buying another. But the size of the transaction is large enough that traders take notice.

Sometimes traders will establish a long or short position (depending on their market view) in advance of the occurrence of one of the imminent events listed above. For example, some traders will establish long (or short) positions in the front month futures contract on Wednesday afternoon in anticipation of the EIA number being released on Thursday morning. In the past, some traders have successfully jammed the EIA website on Thursday mornings (right before the EIA's scheduled release time) by constantly pinging EIA's website hundreds of times every second using automated computer software, thereby causing other traders to be blocked out. But the EIA cracked down upon this malicious activity. Now the website has safeguards to protect against this kind of behavior.

As a trader, natural gas may not be the most valuable commodity you trade. The most valuable commodity today is the data related to natural gas. The trader with the most accurate, actionable, and timely data will be more successful than the uninformed trader.

Bonus Strategy 15: "A" Players Are Free

Annual profit target: $1 million to $5 million

"A" players hire "A" players; "B" players hire "C" players. You want to build your trading organization with people smarter than you. If the head of trading feels threatened by other traders, they may want to hire less experienced traders to protect their turf. This strategy always backfires. Hire and surround yourself with people smarter than you, and then let them do their thing. Build a meritocracy. Award traders based on performance and nothing else. That will automatically attract the best traders to your organization. The superior performance of "A" players more than pays for their compensation packages, thus making "A" players free. "A" players are greedy for one thing: profits. That's who you want in your trading organization. As Michael Douglas's character Gordon Gekko said (paraphrased) in the movie *Wall Street*, "Greed, for lack of a better word, is good. Greed works. Greed has marked the upward ascent of man. And greed, you mark my words, will not only save your company, but it will also save that other malfunctioning corporation called the USA."

Bonus Strategy 16: Asset Light Strategy

Annual profit target: $1 million to $10 million

Some of the strategies mentioned above require a trader to buy actual space on a pipeline and move actual gas molecules from one point to another. But what if a trader does not want to bother with physical gas? There are ways to trade purely financially, that is, without buying an asset such as transport or storage. In fact, there are ways to trade natural gas financially without ever trading the physical gas molecules. Hedge funds usually engage in this strategy so that they do not have to deal with the messy world of physical gas, which involves taking or making delivery of physical gas.

Some of the popular asset light trades involve the trading of financial spreads. For example, in lieu of buying physical storage on a pipeline, you can buy the cheapest futures (let's say October) and sell the most expensive futures contract (let's say January). This effectively mimics buying and injecting cheap gas versus withdrawing and selling high-priced gas. Likewise, to mimic purchasing a transport contract on a pipeline, a trader could simply buy the financial basis contract for the receipt location and sell the financial basis contract for the delivery location. These are cash-settled contracts that do not require the buying or selling of physical gas. So why don't more traders employ this strategy? It's because these strategies are riskier—a lot riskier! We discussed the October–January widow-maker trade in an earlier chapter. This is an example of a pure financial trade. But it bankrupted one hedge fund (Amaranth) to the tune of $6 billion. Trading storage without having actual storage or actual gas is like selling an empty promise. If the market goes against you, you could lose your shirt.

Introduction for Nat Gas Schedulers

Schedulers are wing persons for traders. Traders would not be able to accomplish all their goals without the expertise of schedulers. Schedulers do impactful work every day, and their jobs have a moral purpose. Ensuring the efficient, timely, and reliable delivery of natural gas is critical for energy supply and has a significant impact on both the economy and daily life. After the trader is done consummating the buying or selling of natural gas, they hand over the details of each trade to the scheduler, whose primary job it is to ensure that gas flow occurs in a timely way while minimizing the probability of the gas flow being cut (curtailed) due to pipeline constraints. In the natural gas trading world, you can think of the roles of natural gas traders and schedulers as similar to a sports team's coach and play-caller.

Natural gas traders: Like the head coach of a sports team, natural gas traders are responsible for the overall strategy and big-picture decisions. They analyze market trends, forecast future prices, and make critical decisions on when to buy or sell natural gas to maximize profits. Their role involves a deep understanding of market dynamics, risk management, and economic factors. Traders set the direction and make high-stakes decisions, much like a coach devises game plans and decides on player movements to outmaneuver the competition.

Natural gas schedulers: On the other hand, schedulers are akin to the play-callers or coordinators who execute the coach's game plan. They handle the operational details, ensuring that the natural gas is transported from sellers to buyers efficiently and on time. Schedulers coordinate with pipelines, storage facilities, and other logistical components to manage the physical flow of gas. Their role requires meticulous attention to detail and an ability to adapt quickly to changing circumstances, much like a play-caller who must adjust plays in real time based on the game's progress and unforeseen challenges.

Together, traders and schedulers work in tandem to achieve their team's goals. The trader's strategic vision and market savvy set the stage, while the scheduler's operational expertise and precise execution ensure that the strategy is carried out effectively and efficiently.

Scheduling gas involved submitting a gas nomination (or "nom") to a pipeline. The process of scheduling has evolved over time. A natural gas nomination is a formal request submitted by a market participant (such as a producer, marketer, or trader) to a pipeline company, indicating the quantity of natural gas they intend to transport or receive through the pipeline system over a specified period. This process is crucial for managing the flow of natural gas and ensuring that the supply and demand are balanced across the network. The process of scheduling involves converting trades to noms.

For example, a trader may have executed ten buy trades on ICE. Those ten trades now may need to be chopped up into twenty gas noms across nine different pipelines.

Fifteen noms may involve selling gas to fifteen different counterparties.

Three noms may involve transporting gas over an interruptible transport contract on a pipeline.

One nom may involve transporting gas over a firm transport contract on a pipeline.

One nom may involve injecting gas into a pipeline cavern.

At the end of the whole process, the scheduler has to ensure that all gas going into and out of every pipeline is balanced (this means every receipt MMBtu is matched to every delivered MMBtu of gas) after accounting for fuel loss. If a scheduler makes a data entry mistake, gas may not flow. This makes traders unhappy, because their profits are not realized until gas actually flows and title transfer happens between the buyer and the seller. Let's say a trader bought 10,000 MMBtus of gas and booked a "paper" profit of $1,000 on this trade. The profit is realized only after the gas flows. If only half the gas (5,000 MMBtus) flows, then the trader's profit is cut in half.

In addition to these manual data entry errors, schedulers also have to deal with strict time deadlines. There are five pipeline nomination cycles every day, with a specific time deadline for nom submissions for each cycle. If the deadline is missed, the gas will not flow, which again results in foregone profits. To make things more challenging, pipelines may have constraints in the peak summer and winter months. This means that even if a gas scheduler submitted all noms without data entry errors, gas may still get cut due to pipeline constraints. This is why schedulers need to watch all critical notices posted by pipelines every minute of the day.

It's not humanly possible for traders and schedulers to read every single notice for every single pipeline during the trading hours, during which they are already being constantly bombarded with many other distractions like counterparty instant messages, news events, business meetings, inclement weather, and so much more. This was another reason that I created an automated solution for notices monitoring using artificial intelligence. Now traders and schedulers don't have to read every published critical notice. An AI software reads every notice and informs the trader only in those instances when the software makes a decision that a notice contains some market-moving information. More information about this automated AI notices service can be found here:

https://www.NatGasHub.com/Products

Here are the key components of a natural gas nomination:

Quantity: The amount of natural gas to be transported or received, usually measured in dekatherms (Dth) or metric million British thermal units (MMBtu).

Time period: The specific time frame for the nomination, which can range from hourly to monthly periods, depending on the terms of the contract and the operational requirements.

Receipt and delivery points: The specific locations where the gas will enter (receipt point) and exit (delivery point) the pipeline system.

Contract details: Information about the transportation contract under which the gas will be moved, including contract numbers and service types (for example, firm or interruptible service).

Shipper information: The details of the shipper (the entity submitting the nomination), including contact information and any necessary authorization or verification codes.

The nomination process helps pipeline operators manage the scheduling and allocation of pipeline capacity, ensuring efficient and reliable transportation of natural gas. It also facilitates the coordination between various parties involved in the natural gas supply chain, including producers, marketers, traders, and end-users.

The process of natural gas scheduling has evolved significantly over time due to advances in technology, regulatory changes, and the increasing complexity of the natural gas market. Part of the challenge in scheduling gas lies in the fact that each interstate pipeline is a stand-alone entity regulated by the Federal Energy Regulatory Commission, whose job it is to ensure that all gas shippers are treated equally. This would minimize any favoritism or monopolization of pipeline space. Without proper FERC enforcement, the natural gas pipeline market may become dominated by a few large players who may corner all the space on major pipelines and squeeze small gas producers out of business by not allowing them to access pipeline capacity to bring their product to the market. Each pipeline therefore has created its own unique software and interface, also called an EBB. Pipelines are not allowed to coordinate market activity with one another or collude on pricing. The downside to this is that there is no standard software or interface for each pipeline. In fact, there are myriad nonstandard disparate interfaces across over 300 pipelines in the North American market. This makes it cumbersome for schedulers who must understand the nuances of each pipeline's software.

A scheduler must become an expert in each pipeline's software interface or EBB. This is one of the primary challenges I faced as well as a new entrant into the natural gas industry. I was flabbergasted to learn on my first day on the job that there was not one single interface to communicate with all pipelines. I had handwritten notes from mentors on how to use each pipeline EBB for submitting gas noms. That's when I first got the idea of building one standard interface for schedulers to communicate with all pipes. That idea culminated in a new software being created called NatGasHub.com, which later became the go-to standard in our industry for nominating gas across pipelines. More info about this groundbreaking service can be found here: https://www.NatGasHub.com. Here is an overview of how natural gas scheduling has transformed over the years:

Early Stages (1980 to 2000)

Manual processes: In the early days, natural gas scheduling was a manual process. Schedulers used chalk boards, paper forms, phone calls, and fax machines to coordinate the transportation and delivery of natural gas. This process was time-consuming and prone to errors.

Limited technology: Early technology was rudimentary, with basic computing systems used primarily for record-keeping rather than real-time scheduling. Coordination between producers, pipeline operators, and end-users relied heavily on handshakes, personal communication, and trust.

Introduction of Computer Systems (2001 to 2020)

Basic computerization: As computer technology advanced, basic computer systems were introduced. These systems helped automate some of the record-keeping and communication processes, making scheduling slightly more efficient.

Proprietary software: Pipeline companies began developing proprietary software systems to manage scheduling. These systems provided more structured and reliable ways to track gas flows and manage nominations but were still often isolated and lacked standardization. Most schedulers performed triple entry. The first time they entered all the gas noms into Excel spreadsheets. There were one or more spreadsheets for each pipeline. If you did business across 25 pipes, as an example, you had at least 25 different spreadsheets. Hand typing noms one keystroke at a time was still the primary way of submitting noms to pipelines.

Modern Era (2020 Onward)

Advanced software solutions: The software I created (NatGasHub.com) was launched in the market in 2020. It relies on sophisticated software solutions using a combination of electronic data interchange (EDI) for interstate pipes as well as RPA for intrastate pipes. These systems can standardize over 200 different gas pipeline EBBs into one clean dashboard to automatically submit noms to all pipes without hand-typing. Spreadsheets can also be eliminated entirely. Despite what Excel naysayers have to say, schedulers love Excel spreadsheets. This is why the software can also work seamlessly with Microsoft Excel. It can connect a scheduler's custom Excel spreadsheet directly to the pipeline EBB, thereby eliminating hand-typing of noms.

In November 2022, the popular AI software ChatGPT was born, and it quickly gained traction in the natural gas industry. In 2023, ChatGPT was incorporated into the NatGasHub.com software to allow traders and schedulers to use AI to quickly query pipeline data (like capacity releases, notices, transactional reporting, and more), thereby resulting in increased efficiency in trading and scheduling. These automation software solutions, along with the adoption of AI, have resulted in a paradigm shift in modern gas scheduling capability.

Typically, a scheduler is viewed as a cost by all trading organizations. Scheduling is something that is a necessary function to make gas flow. It is like visiting the gas station. Your primary desire is to keep your vehicle running. But refueling it is a necessary cost in terms of time and money. Scheduling gas is a similar necessary cost in terms of time and money to bring your nat gas commodity from the wellhead to the burner tip. Trading organizations that have become successful over time and those that will survive in the future are the ones that have incorporated the latest technology into their scheduling operations to free up schedulers' time to do more mentally challenging tasks and look for more revenue generating opportunities. They also create work-life balance by allowing schedulers to avoid stress around nom deadlines, hand typing noms, and the loss of revenue due to nom errors.

Integration with trading platforms and ETRMs: Natural gas scheduling systems are now often integrated with trading platforms like ICE as well as ETRMs like Endur, Allegro, FIS, PCI, Enuit, Hitachi, and others, allowing for seamless coordination between trading activities and physical gas flows. This integration helps optimize trading strategies and ensures that scheduled deliveries align with market transactions.

Future Trends

AI and machine learning: The future of natural gas scheduling may see increased use of artificial intelligence and machine learning to further enhance predictive capabilities, optimize scheduling decisions, and reduce operational risks. This is an area on which I plan to devote a majority of my time to further reduce the pain points that still exist and new ones that may crop up in the future in our industry.

Schedulers Who Aspire to Be Traders

Scheduler salaries are typically much lower than trader salaries. Most schedulers are risk-averse but also enjoy higher job security, even if the traders they work for experience large losses. Sometimes, companies may fire a trader who lost a lot of money but keep all the scheduler jobs intact, since the losses were not the result of schedulers' business decisions. Higher risk translates to higher rewards, and vice versa. Scheduler roles are highly sought after because they could be a gateway to future trader jobs.

Scheduler salaries can range from low- to mid-six figures, as well as company benefits. Typically, schedulers will also receive annual bonuses. But unlike traders, the annual bonuses for schedulers are tied to their base salaries, not to trading profits. Here is one example of how an energy trading shop may determine the annual bonus of a natural gas scheduler with seven or more years of experience:

Scheduler annual base salary: $130,000

Scheduler annual benefits package (health, dental, vision, and so on): $15,000

Did trading group meet annual profit target?

If yes, scheduler's bonus is calculated thus:

> For high performers (20 percent to 25 percent): $26,000 to $32,500

For average performers (5 percent to 19 percent): $6,500 to $24,700

For low performers (0 percent): $0

If no, scheduler's bonus is calculated thus:

For high performers (10 percent to 15 percent): $13,000 to $19,500

For average performers (1 percent to 9 percent): $1,300 to $11,700

For low performers (0 percent): $0

A scheduler is considered a high performer if they are able to schedule all pipes on time with no cuts, is a hustler and can identify revenue-generating opportunities for the trader, minimizes pipeline penalties, is always available to schedule gas after hours if needed, can train junior schedulers, is detail-oriented and understands how pipeline constraints work, is a team player and can perform under pressure, completes all nom entries into the company's internal scheduling system daily on time, and maintains a positive attitude throughout the day. As you can see, scheduling is a demanding job. Anytime a scheduler can use technology to ease the workload, it helps them perform better. Here is a rough breakdown of a scheduler's daily activities:

Scheduling gas on various pipeline EBBs: 30 percent

Communicating with schedulers at other companies (counterparties): 20 percent

Completing all nom entries into the company's internal scheduling system: 25 percent

Other activities: 25 percent

I frequently tell all my scheduler friends to continually enhance their skill set to keep up with the times. I ask all schedulers to ask yourself this question: "If I were a cab driver, would I want to be an

Uber driver or a yellow cab driver?" When Uber was born, many yellow cab drivers protested in cities around the world. Those protests all faded away, and Uber and Lyft now dominate the U.S. cab industry. Why did the yellow cab driver protests fail? Was Uber too well funded? The real reason was that these yellow cab drivers were not protesting Uber to begin with. They were protesting against the march of technology. If it wasn't Uber, it would have been some other software company. An "Uber" moment was destined to happen. This is true for any industry, including the natural gas industry.

Those companies that oppose new technologies are really opposing time. Technology is like time. Both march forward constantly in one direction only, and they wait for no person. Technology has represented the upward ascent of humanity. I would encourage all schedulers in our industry to look at technology this way and become early adopters and change evangelists. As the Greek philosopher Heraclitus said, "Change is the only things that's constant in our lives." To look on the bright side, every scheduler could become the go-to technology or AI expert within their own organizations. Just like every company has an Excel expert or an Outlook expert, you could become the AI expert for scheduling. This will elevate your profile within your company as others start seeing you as a leader. It may also rid any fears you may have about AI replacing you. You don't have to have a job title to become a leader. Most leaders start with no titles.

Scheduling is a very important first step to understanding the complex world of natural gas. It is the best place to learn the nuts and bolts of the industry. If you are an existing scheduler who aspires to be a trader or an outsider who aspires to be a trader, here are the things you should focus on to advance to the trader role. I am speaking from experience, as I have personally navigated this transition successfully:

Gain in-depth market knowledge: Understanding the natural gas market dynamics, including supply and demand factors, pricing mechanisms, and market trends, is crucial. Continuous learning through industry publications, market reports, and professional courses can be beneficial.

Develop analytical skills: Traders need strong analytical skills to interpret market data and make informed decisions. Schedulers should focus on improving their ability to analyze complex data, use trading software, and understand financial modeling.

Network within the industry: Building a professional network can open opportunities for mentorship and career advancement. Attending industry conferences, joining professional associations, and participating in networking events can help schedulers connect with experienced traders and industry leaders.

Pursue relevant certifications: Earning certifications such as the chartered financial analyst (CFA) or energy risk professional (ERP) can enhance credibility and demonstrate a commitment to the field.

Seek mentorship: Finding a mentor who is an experienced trader can provide valuable insights, guidance, and support. Mentors can help navigate the complexities of the trading environment and offer advice on career development.

Shadow a trader: Offer to be a backup trader on weekends or when the main trader is on vacation. Many banks have rules that require each trader to be out of the office on a mandatory basis for two weeks each year. During this time, they are not allowed to communicate with any other employee. The purpose of this requirement is to catch any potential rogue unauthorized trading activity that may reside in a trader's portfolio. By offering to be a backup trader, your main trader will start to develop faith in your ability to make trading decisions.

Develop risk-management skills: Understanding and managing risk is a key aspect of trading. Schedulers should familiarize themselves with risk-management principles, tools, and strategies to mitigate potential losses. Buy a book on risk management and study basic concepts such as value-at-risk (VaR), which is the most common tool used to measure the risk of a trader's portfolio.

Improve communication skills: Effective communication is essential for traders who need to convey complex information clearly and make quick decisions. Schedulers should work on enhancing both their written and verbal communication skills.

Gain hands-on experience: Practical experience is invaluable. Schedulers should seek opportunities to work closely with traders, participate in trading simulations, or take on trading-related tasks within their current roles to gain firsthand experience.

Stay informed on regulatory changes: The natural gas market is subject to regulatory changes that can impact trading activities. Staying informed about regulatory updates and compliance requirements is important for aspiring traders.

Show initiative and leadership: Demonstrating a proactive attitude, taking on additional responsibilities, and showing leadership qualities can help schedulers stand out and position themselves for trading roles.

By focusing on these areas, schedulers can build the necessary skills, knowledge, and connections to transition successfully into trading roles.

The Four Nomination Models Every Scheduler Must Know

One of the most important aspects of a scheduler's job is to interact with pipeline EBBs. Every pipeline in North America follows one of these nomination trading models. These are not taught in any school or college and are usually learned by trial and error on the job. At least, that's how it was when I first started scheduling. I wish there were a cheat sheet like the one below in existence when I started. No future scheduler now needs to wish this. The concepts below will help any new entrant into the industry understand these scheduling concepts. Here are the four nomination models every scheduler must know by heart:

Pipeline nomination models:

1. Pathed threaded (PT)
2. Pathed non-threaded (PNT)
3. Non-pathed (NP)
4. Hybrid (H)

Definitions:

Path: A distance along a pipeline from the receipt point (meter) to the delivery point (meter).

Thread: A connection between sequences or chains of nominations that are dependent on one another. In contrast, the term non-threaded means that each nomination is independent and not inherently linked to other nominations. This allows for more flexibility and simplicity, as changes to one nomination do not automatically affect others.

A pipeline usually does not change its nom model. Changing a nom model is a big deal and may require an extensive one-year (or more) technology upgrade by the pipeline. Most schedulers can assume that a pipe's nom model remains the same. A nom model may change when a pipeline gets acquired by another pipeline company and the acquiring company uses a different nom model. This has happened in the past, for example, when Southern Natural Gas (Sonat) pipeline was acquired by Kinder Morgan. Sonat's nom model changed from non-pathed (NP) to pathed non-threaded (PNT). The dominant nom model in the U.S. is pathed threaded (PT). The one used by the fewest number of pipes is non-pathed (NP).

Let's delve into the details of each to see how they work.

A picture speaks a thousand words. Here is a pictorial view of each nom model. If you remember things better with pictures, then think of the PT model as three lines, as shown in the picture below. The PNT model can be thought of as a dumbbell. The NP can be thought of as two pillars. Let me explain what these mean.

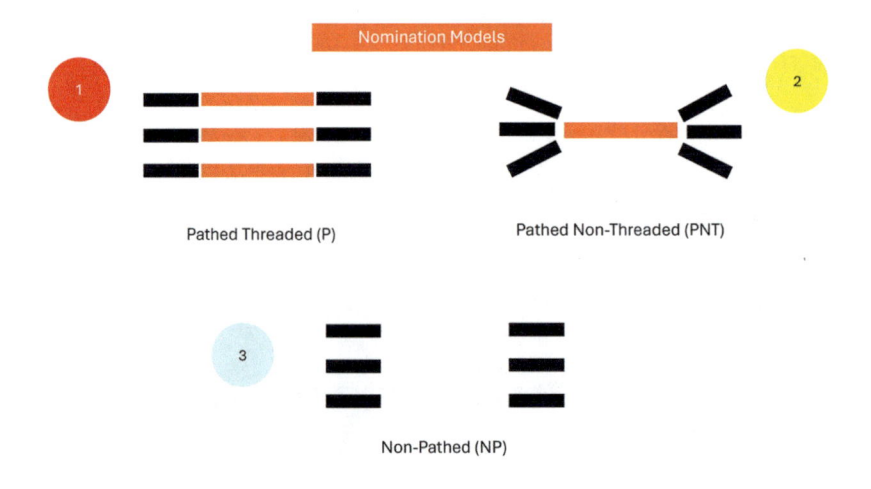

Nomination Models

Pathed Threaded (P)

Pathed Non-Threaded (PNT)

Non-Pathed (NP)

Pathed threaded: This is also simply known as the "pathed" (P) model. I have shown three lines for three sample gas nominations. In this model, each nom is separate and independent from the other lines (noms). It is the simplest of the three nom models shown above, and it is also the least flexible because it treats each nom line item individually and does not allow one nom line item to be tied to another. This means that if you submit 100 pathed noms and one of them is inaccurate, then the 99 accurate ones will still be accepted, whereas the 1 erroneous one would be rejected by the pipeline. In the picture below, gas nomination 1 takes gas from counterparty 1 (CP1) to counterparty 2 (CP2) on path 1 (which could be a firm contract or an interruptible contract). Examples of pipeline families that use this nom model are Enbridge, TC Energy, and Energy Transfer families. Nom 2 takes gas from CP3 and gives it to CP4 on path 2 (contract 2). Nom 1 and nom 2 are completely independent from each other. One can be accepted and the other rejected, or vice versa, by the pipeline. Each nom ties a specific counterparty to another specific counterparty. Think of it as shipping two separate packages on FedEx on the same date. One is from Houston to New York, and another is from Houston to Los Angeles. If one package gets lost or delayed, the other one is unaffected. This is the pathed model for carrying gas on a pipeline.

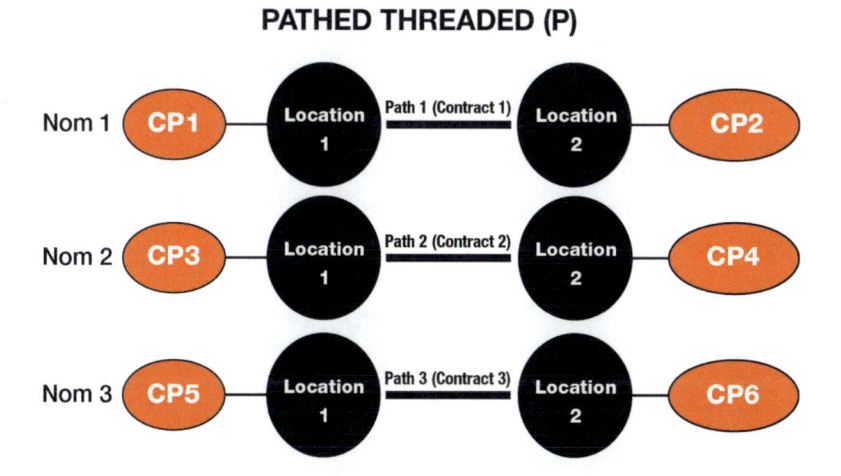

PATHED THREADED (P)

Nom 1: CP1 — Location 1 — Path 1 (Contract 1) — Location 2 — CP2

Nom 2: CP3 — Location 1 — Path 2 (Contract 2) — Location 2 — CP4

Nom 3: CP5 — Location 1 — Path 3 (Contract 3) — Location 2 — CP6

The Four Nomination Models Every Scheduler Must Know

A pathed non-threaded (PNT) model can be thought of as a dumbbell. It is a batch of noms. Each nom in the entire batch must be accurate. If not, the whole batch of noms gets rejected. It's not possible to have only one or a few noms inside the PNT batch be accepted. Examples of pipes that use this nom model (as of the writing of this book) include the Kinder Morgan family of pipes and the Tallgrass family of pipes. In the picture below, all the gas on the left-hand side of the picture (CP1 + CP3 + CP5) from counterparties 1, 3, and 5 can be comingled. All this gas is lumped together and carried on one path (contract) in this example. On the right-hand side of the picture, the gas is disaggregated into three separate packages and sold to three separate counterparties (CP2, CP4, and CP6).

PATHED NON-THREADED (PNT)

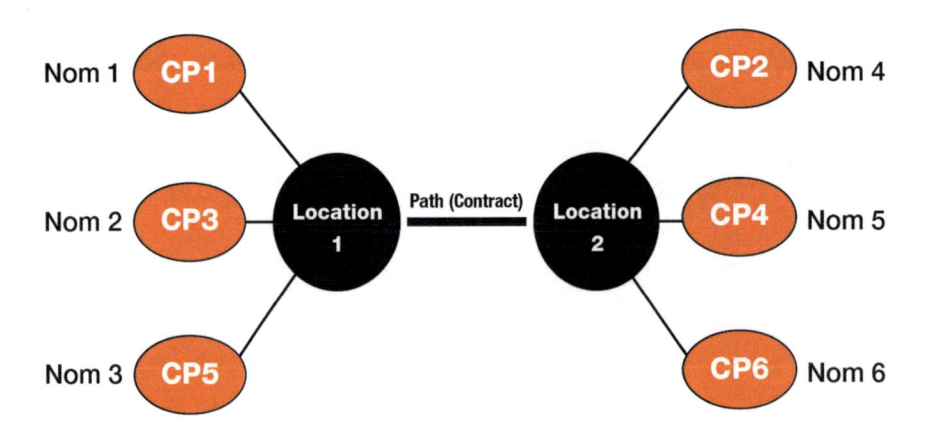

The batch shown above has six threads (three threads on the left and three threads on the right) and one path. Hence, it has a total of seven items.

PATHED NON-THREADED (PNT)

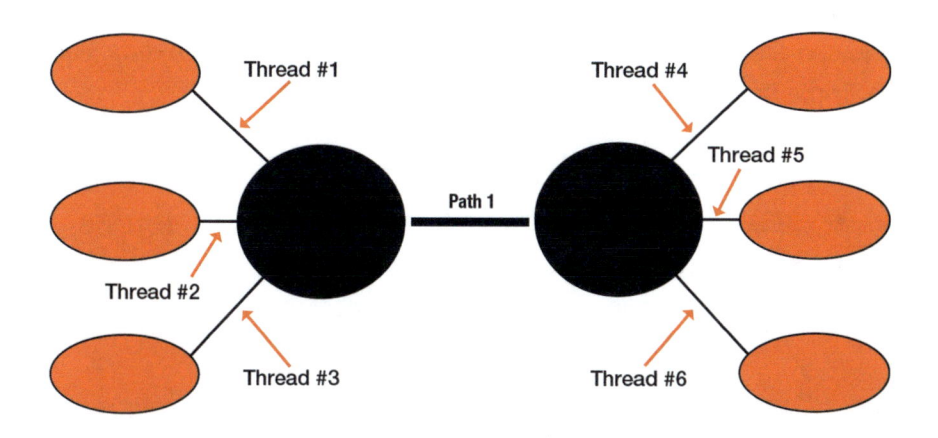

[Diagram: Three supply legs (Thread #1, Thread #2, Thread #3) on the left connect to a black circle, which connects via Path 1 to another black circle, which connects to three market legs (Thread #4, Thread #5, Thread #6) on the right.]

The three threads on the left-hand side are referred to as the supply legs. These are the three companies from whom you are buying or receiving the gas.

The three threads on the right-hand side are referred to as the market legs. These are the three companies to whom you are selling or delivering the gas.

The item in the middle of the image is referred to as the path, or the contract on which you are carrying all the supply packages of gas on the pipeline and delivering to the right-hand side of the pipeline as market. The path connects the supply packages to the market packages. These three pieces together (supply + contract + market) make up the PNT nom batch.

All the supply packages can be comingled among themselves. All the market packages can be comingled among themselves. The pipeline does not force you to tie each supply to each market. Hence, the supply side and the market side are referred to as non-threaded.

The middle section of the picture, the path, is referred to as the pathed segment of the PNT batch. The supply and market portions of the PNT batch are referred to as the non-threaded segments. This is where the name "pathed non-threaded" comes from.

In our example, this batch has a configuration of 3-1-3 (that is, 3 supplies, 1 contract, 3 markets). There are countless scenarios you can create like this one depending on your business needs. For example, here are some possible configurations:

- 3-2-3: 3 supplies + 2 contracts + 3 markets
- 3-3-3: 3 supplies + 3 contracts + 3 markets
- 5-2-7: 5 supplies + 2 contracts + 7 markets
- 9-4-1: 9 supplies + 4 contracts + 1 market

And so on.

Each of these configurations is referred to as a PNT nom batch. There is another requirement for PNT nom batches. The pipelines require you to "fuel-balance" the entire nom batch before you submit the nom batch to the pipeline. If the fuels are not properly calculated by you on each line item, the entire nom batch will be rejected. Even if you have calculated the fuel correctly on all but one of the items in your batch, the entire nom batch will still be rejected. Thus, while the PNT model gives you a lot more flexibility (by giving you the capability to comingle and by not forcing you to tie each item to one item only), the PNT nom batch is also more complicated when it comes to fuel balancing. In the pathed (P) model, you do not have to fuel balance because there is only one nom. Each nom is independent of the other. Let's look at how to accomplish fuel-balancing inside the PNT nom batch. We will look at the same example as before, the 3-1-3 configuration.

Let's say I have 3 supplies of 10,000 MMBtus from counterparty 1 plus 5,000 MMBtus from counterparty 3 plus 8,000 MMBtus from counterparty 5. On each of these 3 supplies, the pipeline charges me 2 percent fuel in-kind to transport the gas from point A to point B. Hence, on the 3 supply packages, I pay a combined fuel of 460 MMBtus. On the right-hand side of the picture, I'm left with 22,540 MMBtus available to sell. I can disaggregate this into any number of market packages and sell them. I choose to disaggregate them into

3 packages of 9,800 MMBtus plus 4,900 MMBtus plus 7,840 MMBtus. The sum of these packages must total exactly 22,540 MMBtus. If not, the batch is not fuel-balanced and will be rejected by the pipe. If I accidentally forget to include the 7,840 package to counterparty 6 in my nom batch (shown in red), then my nom batch is out of balance and will thus be rejected by the pipeline. It is imperative to know the fuel charged on each leg by the pipeline before submitting the nom batch. The fuel percentages can be obtained from the pipeline's tariff, which is posted publicly on its website.

	3 Supplies	1 Contract	3 Markets	
	SUPPLY	CONTRACT	MARKET	
		Contract #1 with Fuel 2%		
Counterparty #1	10,000	(200)	9,800	Counterparty #2
Counterparty #3	5,000	(100)	4,900	Counterparty #4
Counterparty #5	8,000	(160)	7,840	Counterparty #6
	23,000	(460)	22,540	

✓ This batch is fuel-balanced

	3 Supplies	1 Contract	3 Markets	
	SUPPLY	CONTRACT	MARKET	
		Contract #1 with Fuel 2%		
Counterparty #1	10,000	(200)	9,800	Counterparty #2
Counterparty #3	5,000	(100)	4,900	Counterparty #4
Counterparty #5	8,000	(160)	-	Counterparty #6
	23,000	(460)	14,700	

✗ This batch is NOT fuel-balanced

The batch on the top of the picture above is fuel balanced. The same batch is not fuel-balanced if any one of the items is incorrect (as shown in red).

Non-pathed model: An NP model can be thought of as two pillars. It can be made up of one or more supply noms. It could also include one or more market noms. A non-pathed nom batch does not have to have both supply and market. All the supply and market noms are submitted as part of one nom batch to the pipeline. A non-pathed nom batch can consist of one-sided noms only, that is, supply only or market only. It could have many different combinations, as shown below:

- 1 supply + 1 market
- 1 supply + 2 markets
- 3 supplies + 5 markets

- 1 supply
- 2 markets
- 1 market
- 9 supplies + 6 markets

And so on.

The sum of all the supply noms must equal the sum of all the market noms. If not, the entire nom batch will be rejected by the pipe. This nom model is not used by many pipes in the market. As of the writing of this book, some of the pipes that use this nom model include ANR and Transco pipeline.

Hybrid (H) nom model: This nom model by itself does not exist as a stand-alone nom model. Whenever a pipe uses a hybrid nom model, it means the pipeline uses any two of the nom models (that is, P, PNT, or NP). An example of this type of pipe is Iroquois pipeline, which is a hybrid pipe using both the PNT and NP nom models. The different nom models are used by the same pipe to signify different transaction types. For example, ANR is a hybrid pipeline that uses both P as well as NP nom models. For firm transport nominations (transaction type = 01), ANR uses a P model. For pool noms (transaction type = 08), ANR uses an NP model. A list of all the nom models for each pipeline in North America is available for paying subscribers of the NatGasHub.com software by emailing GasPro@NatGasHub.com.

Some more advanced terms in scheduling are listed here:

311 Pipeline: This refers to a natural gas pipeline that operates under section 311 of the Natural Gas Policy Act of 1978 (NGPA). These pipelines are typically intrastate pipelines, meaning they operate within a single state's borders and are regulated by that state's public utility commission. However, section 311 allows these intrastate pipelines to transport natural gas on behalf of interstate pipelines or local distribution companies (LDCs) in interstate commerce, subject to regulations set by FERC.

The following are key characteristics of 311 pipelines:

Intrastate operation: Primarily operate within the boundaries of a single state.

Interstate service authorization: Authorized under section 311 to provide transportation services for interstate commerce without being fully subject to FERC's comprehensive regulation applicable to interstate pipelines.

Rate regulation: Rates for services under Section 311 must be fair and equitable and are subject to FERC approval to ensure they are just and reasonable.

Limited FERC oversight: While FERC regulates the transportation rates and terms of service for the interstate transactions, the pipelines remain primarily under state jurisdiction for other aspects of their operations.

Meter bounce: In the U.S. natural gas market, a meter bounce refers to the practice of briefly diverting natural gas through an intermediate meter or point before delivering it to its final destination. This maneuver is often used for accounting, measurement, or contractual purposes. It provides operational flexibility for pipeline operators and shippers to manage flows and balance supply and demand more effectively.

Predetermined allocation (PDA): Is a contractual arrangement that specifies in advance how natural gas quantities will be allocated among different parties at a shared point of delivery or receipt. This arrangement is used to streamline and simplify the allocation process, ensuring clarity and reducing potential disputes. Key aspects of a PDA include the following:

Advance agreement: Allocation percentages or volumes are agreed upon before the gas flows, based on contractual terms.

Allocation point: PDAs are applied at specific points in the pipeline network where multiple shippers or parties have an interest in the gas being delivered or received.

Automated allocation: The predetermined percentages or volumes are automatically applied when gas flows, facilitating efficient and accurate distribution of gas among the parties.

Flexibility and transparency: PDAs provide flexibility in gas management and enhance transparency, as all parties are aware of their allocated shares beforehand.

PDAs are commonly used to manage complex transportation and storage agreements, improving operational efficiency and ensuring that each party receives its correct share of the gas.

Elapsed prorated scheduled quantity (EPSQ): Refers to the method used to determine the proportional amount of natural gas that should have been delivered or received up to a specific point in time within a gas day, based on the originally scheduled quantity. This calculation is essential for managing imbalances and adjustments in gas flows. Key aspects of EPSQ include the following:

Proportional allocation: EPSQ calculates the quantity of gas that should have flowed proportionally based on the time elapsed within the gas day.

Scheduling adjustments: These help in making adjustments to scheduled quantities when there are changes in nominations, interruptions, or curtailments. EPSQ prevents a gas scheduler from cutting a nomination volume below a volume that has already flowed. In other words, pipelines don't allow a scheduler to undo the gas that has already flowed. This is like dropping a letter in the mail.

Imbalance management: This assists shippers and pipeline operators in managing imbalances by providing a clear benchmark for the expected flow versus the actual flow.

Operational accuracy: This ensures accurate and fair allocation of gas, especially in cases where the gas day is not fully completed or where there are midday scheduling changes.

EPSQ is a critical tool for maintaining the integrity and balance of natural gas transportation systems, ensuring that all parties have a consistent and fair reference for the amounts of gas that should have been delivered or received during any part of the gas day.

Operational balancing agreement (OBA): Is a contract between a pipeline and a shipper. The OBA outlines the procedures and responsibilities for balancing the amount of gas scheduled and the amount of gas actually delivered or received. Key aspects of an OBA include the following:

Balancing responsibilities: This is the process of defining the responsibilities of each party for managing and rectifying gas imbalances that occur at the interconnection point.

Reconciliation procedures: This establishes the procedures for measuring, tracking, and reconciling discrepancies between scheduled and actual gas flows.

Tolerance levels: This specifies acceptable levels of imbalance, often with predefined limits within which imbalances can occur without penalty.

Settlement terms: These detail the financial or operational settlement terms for imbalances, including any penalties or charges for exceeding tolerance levels.

Operational coordination: This ensures operational coordination between the parties to maintain system reliability and integrity, facilitating efficient gas flow management.

Get your scheduling cheat sheet here:

https://www.NatGasHub.com/SchedulingCheatSheet

Cracking the Code on Pipeline Tariffs

Pipeline tariffs are the prices pipelines charge shippers to move gas on their pipes from one location to another. For interstate pipelines, each tariff item must be approved by the Federal Energy Regulatory Commission before the pipelines can roll it out to the market and start charging shippers. Intrastate pipeline tariffs do not fall under the purview of the FERC. They are regulated and approved by various local government entities. For instance, the Texas intrastate pipeline market is regulated by the Texas Railroad Commission. Yes, you read that right—the Railroad Commission!

The primary mandate of the FERC when it comes to natural gas tariffs is to ensure they are just, reasonable, and nondiscriminatory. FERC monitors and investigates the natural gas markets to prevent market manipulation and ensure fair competition. At the same time, FERC understands that natural gas pipelines are for-profit companies. Hence, FERC approves pipeline tariffs in such a way that it allows pipelines to make a fair rate of return on their investment. Any time a pipeline would like to charge more by increasing its tariff, it must first obtain FERC approval. In its FERC filing, a pipeline would need to justify the reason it is seeking a rate increase. FERC allows a public comment period during which any shipper may raise an objection against the tariff increase with a reasonable basis. FERC commissioners would then review both sides of the argument (pipeline versus shipper) and make a ruling whether to grant the tariff increase or deny it.

The rate of return the FERC considers reasonable for natural gas pipelines typically falls within a range determined through a detailed evaluation process. This evaluation includes considering the pipeline company's cost of debt, cost of equity, and overall capital structure. Historically, the rate of return on equity (ROE) for natural gas pipelines approved by FERC has often been in the range of 10 to 14 percent. FERC's goal is to ensure the rate of return is sufficient to attract investment in necessary infrastructure while protecting consumers from excessive rates.

Some pipeline tariffs are very simple, and some are extremely complicated. To a new entrant in the industry, understanding pipeline tariffs can be daunting. In this regard, the pipeline industry is similar to the healthcare industry, where there are so many different types of healthcare plans that most people may not understand them. But since healthcare is a necessity, most people end up paying the lowest healthcare premiums they can find without understanding whether their plans will cover them when they fall sick. This chapter will help you understand tariffs so that you don't ever buy space on a pipeline and end up in a situation where you can't flow the gas because you didn't understand the tariffs and your rights as a pipeline shipper.

Whether a pipeline's tariff is simple or complicated depends on what type of services the pipeline offers and how vast its infrastructure is. A pipeline that only offers transport service, for example, may have a very simple tariff structure, like Southern Star Pipeline, for example. Pipelines that offer transport, storage, and parks and loans, as well as connecting to an LNG facility or power plants, may have a very complex tariff structure with many different tariff rate schedules for each type of service. An example of this is Transcontinental pipeline. Some pipelines charge a flat rate from one point to another, while others offer a mileage-based tariff that can become quite complicated. An example of a mileage-based tariff pipeline is Northern Border.

A pipeline tariff consists of four major components:

1. Reservation (demand) charge: This is a fixed charge.
2. Commodity rate: This is a variable charge.
3. Fuel rate: This is a variable charge.
4. Annual charge adjustment (ACA): This is a fixed charge for the whole year but changes once per year.

Reservation (demand) charge: This is a fixed charge per MMBtu per month charged by the pipeline, regardless of whether the shipper flows the gas or not. Pipelines charge this for firm service (as opposed to interruptible). *Firm* implies that a shipper has the right but not the obligation to flow gas. I mentioned earlier that pipelines are like airlines. *Interruptible* is akin to flying standby on an airplane. You can reserve space on a pipeline just like you book a seat on an airline. You may not end up actually flowing the gas (or flying on the plane). But just the fact you could reserve space has some value. Pipelines call this the reservation charge or demand charge. It is a sunk cost, and you must pay it regardless of whether you decide to flow the gas or not.

Commodity rate: This is a variable charge per MMBtu per month charged by the pipeline only if the shipper flows the gas. Pipelines charge this for both firm as well as interruptible service. It is a variable charge because the charge actually depends upon the volume of gas that the shipper elects to flow.

Fuel (or retention) rate (or percentage): This is a variable charge by the pipeline only if the shipper flows the gas. It is charged as a percentage of the volume of gas that is flowed. This charge is not a cash charge. In fact, it is paid in-kind to the pipeline. The way the pipeline bills for this charge is that it retains (confiscates) a portion the gas the shipper actually flows on the pipeline. Pipelines charge this in-kind fuel for both firm as well as interruptible service. For example, for a 2 percent fuel rate charged by the pipeline, if a shipper provides 10,000 MMBtus of gas to the pipeline at the receipt meter (or location), then the pipeline will retain 2 percent of the 10,000 MMBtus (that is, 200 MMBtus) and allow the shipper to take the remaining 9,800 MMBtus at the delivery meter (location).

Annual charge adjustment (ACA): The ACA is a fee assessed by the FERC to recover the costs of its regulatory program. It normally fluctuates very little (in the range of $0.0001 to $0.0005 per MMBtu per year). The ACA charge is calculated and published by the FERC to be effective on October 1 of the current year and stay in effect until October 1 of the following year. Currently, it is $0.0015 per MMBtu. Since the absolute amount of the ACA and the amount it fluctuates by from year to year are so small, most traders do not consider it material enough to include in their profit and loss trading calculations.

Let's work through an example:

A shipper owns 10,000 MMBtus of firm transport (rate schedule FTS-1) on ANR Pipeline for the month of July from the primary receipt point of ANR Southeast Head station (in Louisiana) to the primary delivery point of ANR Joliet Hub (near Chicago). The pipeline's tariff states the reservation charge for ANR Southeast Area to the ML-7 (Joliet Hub) is $14.8516 per MMBtu per month (as shown in the chart below). Let's convert this to a daily basis, because we trade gas one flow day at a time. This monthly charge of $14.8516 equates to a daily charge of $0.479 per MMBtu per day, accounting for 31 days in the month of July.

Right below the reservation charge in the same table below is displayed the Commodity (Cmd) charge for this route, which is $0.0356 per MMBtu per day. The "Ovrn" commodity charge applies only if I exceed (overrun) my allotted volume or quantity of 10,000 MMBtus per day (this is referred to as my maximum daily quantity, or MDQ). We will ignore the overrun charge, because I do not plan to exceed my allotted quantity.

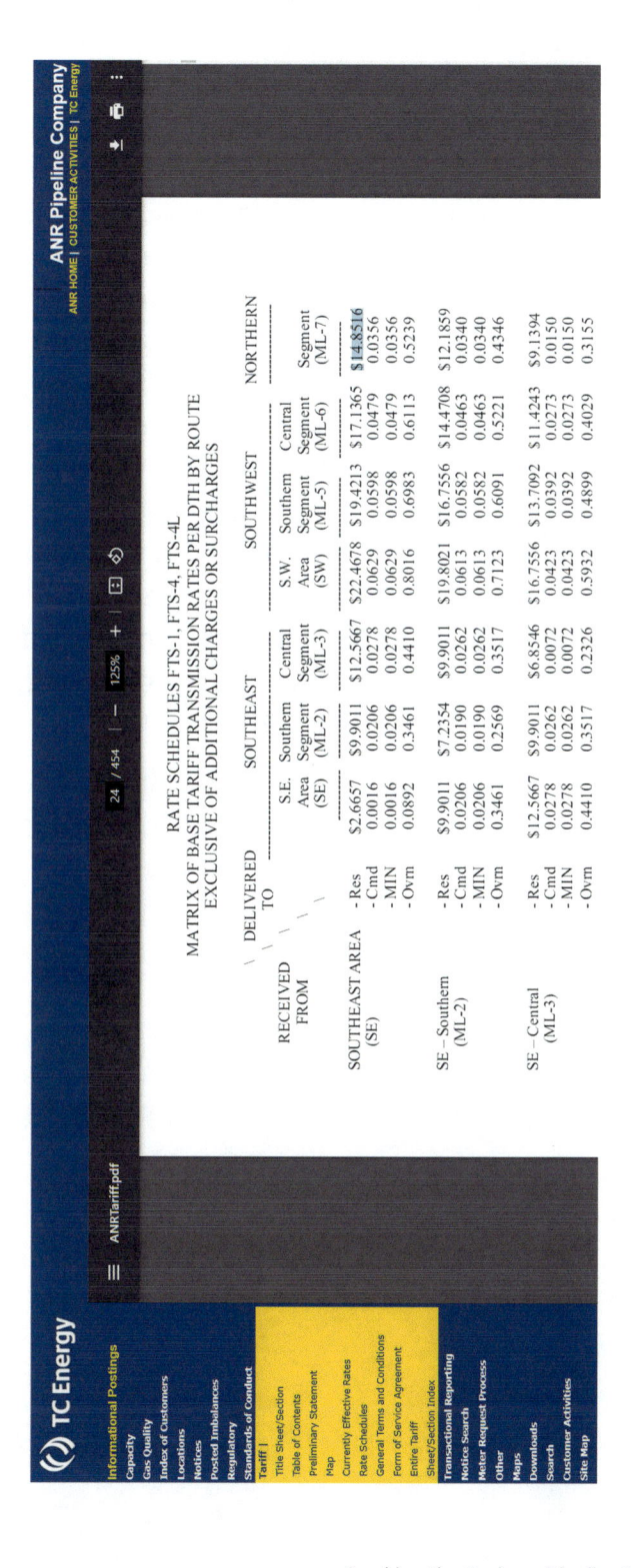

RATE SCHEDULES FTS-1, FTS-4, FTS-4L
MATRIX OF BASE TARIFF TRANSMISSION RATES PER DTH BY ROUTE
EXCLUSIVE OF ADDITIONAL CHARGES OR SURCHARGES

RECEIVED FROM	DELIVERED TO		SOUTHEAST			SOUTHWEST			NORTHERN
		S.E. Area (SE)	Southern Segment (ML-2)	Central Segment (ML-3)	S.W. Area (SW)	Southern Segment (ML-5)	Central Segment (ML-6)	Segment (ML-7)
SOUTHEAST AREA (SE)	-Res	$2.6657	$9.9011	$12.5667	$22.4678	$19.4213	$17.1365	$14.8516
	-Cmd	0.0016	0.0206	0.0278	0.0629	0.0598	0.0479	0.0356
	-MIN	0.0016	0.0206	0.0278	0.0629	0.0598	0.0479	0.0356
	-Ovr	0.0892	0.3461	0.4410	0.8016	0.6983	0.6113	0.5239
SE – Southern (ML-2)	-Res	$9.9011	$7.2354	$9.9011	$19.8021	$16.7556	$14.4708	$12.1859
	-Cmd	0.0206	0.0190	0.0262	0.0613	0.0582	0.0463	0.0340
	-MIN	0.0206	0.0190	0.0262	0.0613	0.0582	0.0463	0.0340
	-Ovr	0.3461	0.2569	0.3517	0.7123	0.6091	0.5221	0.4346
SE – Central (ML-3)	-Res	$12.5667	$9.9011	$6.8546	$16.7556	$13.7092	$11.4243	$9.1394
	-Cmd	0.0278	0.0262	0.0072	0.0423	0.0392	0.0273	0.0150
	-MIN	0.0278	0.0262	0.0072	0.0423	0.0392	0.0273	0.0150
	-Ovr	0.4410	0.3517	0.2326	0.5932	0.4899	0.4029	0.3155

Cracking the Code on Pipeline Tariffs | 161

We've figured out the reservation charge and the commodity charge. Now let's look in the ANR tariff for the fuel charge. From the table below, you can see ANR charges a fuel percentage of 2.05 percent. Let's assume that I'm flowing 10,000 MMBtus in this example. Hence, my fuel loss (the volume that ANR will retain) is 200 MMBtus (that is, 2 percent of my receipt volume). I need to convert this 2 percent charge to a dollar amount. This is because I need to see all my charges in the same units: dollars per MMBtu per day. Since my reservation and commodity charges are expressed in dollars per MMBtu per day, my fuel percentage charge also needs to be converted to the same basis. The way to do this is to look for the price of gas being traded in the market at the location of ANR Southeast Head station. This is the receipt location where I'll be buying my gas. I can find this price on ICE (Intercontinental Exchange). Let's say this price is $3.25 per MMBtu. Thus, my fuel charge will be 2 percent of $3.25, which is equal to $0.065 per MMBtu.

TRANSPORTER'S USE (%)

1. Transporter's Use (%) for all transmission Transportation Services in Volume Nos. 1 and 2:

FROM: \ TO:	SOUTHEAST (PERCENTAGE)			SOUTHWEST			NORTHERN
	S.E. Area (SE)	Southern Segment (ML-2)	Central Segment (ML-3)	S.W. Area (SW)	Southern Segment (ML-5)	Central Segment (ML-6)	Segment (ML-7)
SOUTHEAST AREA (SE)	0.70	1.37	1.84	3.86	3.18	2.76	2.05
S.E. SOUTHERN SEGMENT (ML-2)	1.37	0.82	1.29	3.31	2.63	2.21	1.50
S.E. CENTRAL SEGMENT (ML-3)	1.84	1.29	0.62	2.64	1.96	1.54	0.83
SOUTHWEST AREA (SW)	3.86	3.31	2.64	0.83	1.25	1.96	2.17

Cracking the Code on Pipeline Tariffs | 163

Now we have all the charges we need:

Reservation cost = $0.479/MMBtu

Commodity cost = $0.0356/MMBtu

Fuel cost = $0.065/MMBtu

ACA cost = $0.0015/MMBtu

Total cost = $0.5796

Let's say the price of gas trading in the market is as follows:

ANR Southeast Head station (receipt location) = $3.25/MMBtu

ANR Joliet Hub ML7 Zone (delivery location) = $4.25/MMBtu

Price spread = $4.25 − $3.25 = $1.00/MMBtu

The gross profit for flowing gas on one day is calculated as follows:

Gross profit = ($1.00 − $0.5796) × 10,000 MMBtus = $4,204

Pipelines can change their tariff at any time after getting FERC approval. Several pipelines will update their fuel and commodity rates twice per year (on April 1 for the summer season, and again on October 1 or November 1 for the winter season). Some pipes update their fuel percentages monthly. Hence, a trader should be monitoring all FERC legal dockets in order to not be blindsided by surprise tariff changes. A trader's forward profit or loss is affected if the pipeline revises its fuel or commodity charges up or down. As traders are making their daily buy and sell decisions, they have the tariffs on all their pipes memorized. Tariffs are a source of risk because when you buy transport or storage space on a pipeline, the fuel percentages and commodity rates can change after you consummate the deal. These tariffs are also captured in a trader's deal entry system (trade capture system) in order to calculate the correct profit or loss at the end of each day. Monitoring, scraping, and hand-typing tariffs into your company's trade capture system is a major pain point for every gas shipper.

I experienced this pain personally when I was a gas trader. In order to eliminate this pain point, I created an automated tariffs service using AI that would automatically update all tariff changes for all pipes directly into a shipper's trade capture system. This was a paradigm shift in how tariffs are being managed by all traders and schedulers in the market today. Even pending tariffs can be automatically monitored and updated using this software. More info about this product can be found here:

https://www.NatGasHub.com/Tariffs

Introduction for Nat Gas Technologists

In the rapidly evolving landscape of natural gas trading, where volatility is the norm and margins can be razor-thin, the role of technology has never been more pivotal. As a technologist in a natural gas trading company, you stand at the forefront of this transformation. You are uniquely positioned to harness two types of powerful technologies that we will explore in the next two chapters: (1) the power of AI, and (2) robotic process automation (RPA) to drive unprecedented profits and efficiencies in the U.S. natural gas markets.

Imagine a world where trading decisions are based not just on historical data and gut feelings but on real-time analytics and predictive algorithms. Picture your trading floor where mundane and repetitive tasks are handled flawlessly by intelligent bots, freeing your team to focus on strategic decision-making and innovation. This is not a distant future; it is the reality today.

As a technologist, you already understand the immense potential of AI and RPA. These technologies are not just tools; they are catalysts for revolutionizing how we approach trading. AI, with its ability to analyze vast datasets and identify patterns invisible to the human eye, can predict market movements with astonishing accuracy. RPA, on the other hand, can automate complex workflows, ensuring that trades are executed with precision and speed, and compliance requirements are met without error. Your expertise in these areas gives you a competitive edge. You have the knowledge and the capability to implement systems that can transform trading operations, reduce risks, and increase profitability. This chapter is your guide to leveraging that expertise to its fullest potential.

By integrating these technologies into your trading strategy, you can turn potential obstacles into strategic advantages. This chapter will show you how to develop and implement AI models tailored to the nuances of the natural gas market. It will guide you through the process of deploying RPA to optimize your trading operations, from data entry to settlement. Welcome to the new frontier of natural gas trading. Let's embark on this exciting journey together and transform challenges into opportunities and potential into profit.

Where to Implement AI in Your Organization

The short answer to this question is "Where there is a pain point?" I'll illustrate with a simple example. I was doing my taxes last weekend. I had 24 credit card statements in PDF format. I needed to put them all into Excel to try and separate my personal expenses from my business expenses. I was scratching my head about how to do this quickly. It would have taken me about an hour and a half. Instead, I uploaded them into ChatGPT and typed a simple command—in English. I didn't even have to write any code! ChatGPT converted all those 24 credit card statements into one Excel file with all charges organized by month. This is a job that might have been done by a tax consultant, perhaps someone at Jackson Hewitt. But now that job is gone forever. Because neither do I want to do it, nor does my tax consultant want to do it. Now there is a software that does this better, faster, and cheaper. This job is gone forever!

There are many white-collar jobs like this one that are being eliminated every day. And I think that causes anxiety for a lot of people, because people think, "Will AI eliminate my job?" I don't want to sugarcoat anything. There will certainly be jobs lost. But there are simultaneously jobs being created. In this example about the credit card statements, 90 minutes of someone's job got eliminated forever. But the job being created is that now more electricity is being consumed by AI models. The difference in electricity is nine times. When you ask a question on Google search versus posing the same question to ChatGPT, nine times more energy is consumed by ChatGPT. This is because the language learning model (LLM) inside ChatGPT is crunching more numbers (by using more electricity) to give you a better answer. A traditional Google search couldn't give me one consolidated neat spreadsheet for all my credit card statements with all the numbers organized. But ChatGPT can. This is the technology of the future!

The first step to implementing AI within your organization is to identify someone's pain point. It should be a small, manual, repetitive task that takes an employee a few hours to do every day. Let's use a real example from the natural gas world: monitoring and updating pipeline tariffs into your energy trading and risk management system. It takes each scheduler anywhere from 30 minutes to an hour every day to manually monitor and update tariffs. The task involves reading lengthy 500-page PDF documents on every pipeline's website, which a scheduler must monitor. Typically, schedulers are handling five to ten pipes each. So they must monitor five to ten different websites and scrape the tariff data manually. Since they do not know when a pipeline's tariff may change, they also have to scour the notices section of every pipe's website or the FERC website to determine if the pipeline has filed a legal docket to change their tariff. This is a cumbersome process. If the pipeline has changed some tariff line item, then the scheduler must log into the company's ETRM system and manually hand-type the new tariff data. This is also a laborious, boring, time-consuming task.

Good news! AI was built specifically to solve this kind of problem. An AI software can read and understand (because it has a language learning model) literally hundreds of documents across hundreds of websites and neatly summarize the changes for you in a standardized format. Once the AI software provides you the standardized tariff changes across five to ten pipes, it eliminates the pain point of you having to go out and manually scrape tariffs.

The next task is to update these tariffs into your ETRM system. That is different task than reading and summarizing a tariff. For uploading a tariff into a system, you can employ a different technology called RPA, which is discussed in the next section. The automation of this tariff task can be achieved using a combination of both AI software as well as RPA software. The AI software will read and summarize the tariff data. The RPA software will perform the task of data entry. Think of it as two tasks: one done by your brain (reading the tariff), and the other done by your hand (typing the tariff into your ETRM). AI does the brain work. RPA does the hand work. This frees up humans from having to do any work. To view the different kinds of ready-made AI-infused products available for the natural gas industry, please visit this link:

https://www.NatGasHub.com/Products

This is the framework you should use for achieving a high level of automation for any pain point in your organization for any employee. Keep shaving off 30 minutes to an hour of someone's daily time. That frees them up to do more mentally challenging tasks, such as learning how the new AI software works, learning how the new RPA software works, or using the time savings to generate new revenue for your company. This automation will lead to lower employee stress, lower turnover, enhanced employee skills, and higher job satisfaction.

Rinse and repeat for the next pain point!

RPA: Welcome to the Age of Digital Labor

What is RPA, or robotic process automation? The definition lies more in the term *process automation* and less in actual robots. But RPA is changing the world much like physical robots have. Let's take the example of an employee named Nate, who has to scrape data from a number of different websites multiple times a day by downloading files in different formats like PDF, CSV, Word, and so on, and then converting them into one clean standardized Excel spreadsheet format. Then, he has to perform calculations on some of the columns in the spreadsheet to manipulate some data, for example, adding four Excel columns to create a new subtotal column. Then, he has to upload the resultant file into an in-house ETRM system. And finally, he has to email the same file to multiple internal employees. Let's say he has to do this three times a day, every day, which consumes 2,190 hours per year!

Nate's very unhappy about this because it's a tedious, repetitive, mind-numbing task, prone to errors. But using RPA, he could automate this task as follows: Nate has to extract data from third-party websites. This is one of the places RPA can be combined with an AI software such as ChatGPT, which uses a LLM. An AI software can intelligently read the content on a website and even download files and read the data inside those files. This data is extracted for further processing. This data could include things like the meter numbers on a natural gas pipeline across the entire continent of

North America, how much volume of gas is flowing through each meter, and so on. The AI software then hands the data in a clean, standardized format to the RPA software, which validates the data to ensure nothing is corrupt and that all the data looks good. Once the data is cleansed and standardized, then the RPA software performs some predetermined calculations provided by Nate and maybe adds new rows or columns into the combined data spreadsheet. Then the RPA software uses Nate's credentials to log into the ETRM system and upload the data into the ETRM. Finally, the RPA job will email the same Excel spreadsheet to 30 different email recipients as an attachment. This is how RPA helps by automating tedious repetitive tasks that require clicking through multiple user interfaces, copying and pasting data, and uploading, downloading, or inserting data from one website or system into another.

Ask yourself these three questions in order to decide whether a manual task is ripe for automation using RPA:

1. Is the task repetitive?
2. Is the task manual?
3. Does the task involve no or very little decision-making?

If the answer to the three questions above is yes, then that manual task is a good candidate for RPA. The hours saved can be translated into profits for your company. All RPA jobs should be well publicized to your management so that you receive the recognition and annual compensation incentives for reducing your company's labor costs.

When choosing an RPA system that would enable you to do this type of automation, there are three major things that you need to be looking for:

1. **Intelligent:** The first thing is you want to make sure your RPA tool is intelligent. In this example, Nate combined AI with RPA, then used different data manipulation

techniques, and even emailed an Excel file to other coworkers. This is just the tip of the iceberg of what RPA can do. RPA can be combined with AI and machine learning (ML) software.
2. **No code:** Nate is not a developer. Find an RPA service provider that can build and maintain this RPA bot for you so Nate doesn't have to. Your core business may not be software development. Maintaining a piece of code is not something you should have to do, because it erodes the RPA benefit by simply transferring Nate's job to another employee. Find a solution that offers RPA as a service. This way, the company that built the RPA job for you will ensure the RPA job runs to completion without fail every day.
3. **Concurrency:** This is the ability to run multiple robots at the same time. This frees up many more employees like Nate within your organization to focus on more mentally challenging and revenue generating tasks.

This was a quick overview of RPA. RPA is quickly growing in popularity, and so is the scope of what RPA is able to actually automate. For more information, visit

https://www.NatGasHub.com/AutomationHub

The Top Five Traits of High Earners in the Nat Gas Industry

For this book, I interviewed the best performers (traders, schedulers, and technologists) in the nat gas industry. I define high performers as those who have moved up the corporate ladder with greater speed and success than others while multiplying their take-home pay two to ten times over their careers.

Let me start with something you will find shocking. All of us, including all the high performers, are lazy. Yes, you heard that right—lazy! High performers are lazy too. However, high performers have done something about it. They have worked hard to build the systems, rituals, and processes to protect themselves from their own laziness. In their work lives, they are intensely disciplined. Outside those areas, they're lazy. I noticed this dichotomy among all the high performers I interviewed. They have intentionally built routines and habits to achieve success despite their laziness. You can build these habits too! When I understood this pattern, I realized two things. First, their success has less to do with their inborn talents, intelligence, nature, and so on. Their success was simply a result of the process they built into their lives to create and reinforce successful habits. That's something anyone can do! Second, I realized how critically important building great habits is.

Here's why developing good habits is so crucially important and why doing this can increase your take-home pay. Approximately 95 percent of your organic habits are unconscious. This means you are essentially sleepwalking through your workday. You're not consciously aware of about 95 percent of the decisions you make and the behavior that follows. Let me give you an example. Do you remember when you were first learning to drive a car? You were told to keep your hands at 10 and 2 o'clock, check your rearview mirror regularly, check the left mirror, test your indicators, tap your right foot for the gas and left foot for the brake, and so on. It seemed impossible. But today you can do all those things while listening to the radio and checking your phone for directions. You don't even have to think about driving. Why? Because it has all become automatic. It has become a learned habit. When you repeat an action over and over again, it creates a neuro signature in your brain. Habits start out like cobwebs. Then they become cables. Breaking your bad habits is as mentally, emotionally, and physically challenging as it is for someone to break the habit of substance abuse.

To determine good habits, it comes down to your goals. Let's say your goal is to double your take-home pay. What's the most important thing to help you achieve this goal? You might be inclined to say it is closing twice as many new transactions. For that, you may need to double the time you spend prospecting for new gas clients. That's the new habit you need to create: spending more time prospecting. Next, you eliminate the bad habits keeping you from practicing the good habit you just created. Therefore, scrolling through social media, watching YouTube videos, online shopping, and anything else that distracts you from your good habit is your bad habit.

How do you uproot bad habits? Here's the good news about bad habits. All habits are learned. When you were born, you had no habits. You were a clean slate. Thus, if you have learned something, you can unlearn it too.

Here are the top five traits of high earners in the nat gas industry:

1. They remove the triggers of bad habits. What is something that happens before your bad habit activates? Use the four Ws: who, when, what, where. Who triggers your bad habit? Maybe it's a friend who invites you to lunch. When does your bad habit get triggered? Perhaps it's on Friday when you realize you haven't accomplished your goal for that week. What triggers your bad habit? Maybe it's the fear of being rejected by a prospective client. Where does your bad habit get triggered? May be it's when you're working from home or from the office. Once you know the triggers, take actions to turn them off before they attack.
2. Multitasking is their enemy. Do focused work, not multitasking. Identify the one daily task that is most important for your take-home pay. For traders, it's your profit for today. Period. For a scheduler, it may be ensuring 100 percent of gas flows for today without any errors. For a technologist, it may be that 99.99 percent of your company's software applications run without interruption today. Avoid useless meetings, pointless phone calls, and YouTube videos that distract you from your most important task. In your annual performance review, have your boss agree to the one most important task that will determine your annual year-end bonus. For traders, a majority of your eight-hour day must be spent maximizing your profit. Let's say your assigned profit target is $5,000 for today and gets reported at 4 p.m. Work backward. Eliminate every task and distraction that will get in the way. And yes, multitasking is also a distraction! Vital work is different from trivial work. Your vital work is generating profits. Your trivial work is phone calls, emails, training sessions, administrative tasks, and any other

fluff that gives the appearance of making you look busy. Don't hide behind trivial work. Eliminate it. Multitasking is your enemy. Busy does not equal productive. Busy only gives you a dopamine hit by tricking you into thinking you're important. I call this the rocking-horse syndrome. You're rocking, but you're not getting anywhere. Most professionals spend their entire careers this way and get nowhere. Identify your one most important daily goal. If you don't have that, you're lost. And if you don't know where you're going, anywhere will get you there.

3. They break a herculean task into smaller tasks. Only look at the next step on your ladder. Don't look at the entire ladder. Set up audacious goals with a deadline. Then work backward and break them down into small, bite-size tasks. When you wake up in the morning, you may feel overwhelmed that you have to climb a mountain. But if you trained your mind the night before that you only need to take three steps tomorrow to climb the mountain, you can accomplish your daily goal. This will eliminate the procrastination you've been allowing to creep into your career.

4. They practice the art of delegation. People think of high achievers as control freaks and perfectionists. One of the most highly paid managers at a gas trading company said that delegation is the most important reason for her success. But she can't delegate to just anyone. Her skill lies in delegating the right task to the right people on her team. The importance of delegation is frequently quoted by many successful professionals in the nat gas industry. It is the one habit that will free up your time to help you achieve your most important goal. Now that you have identified your most important task at work for this quarter (for example, making a profit, ensuring 100 percent of gas flows without errors every day, assuring 99.99 percent of software availability, and so on), all your other tasks need

to be delegated effectively so that no one drops the ball. If one of your most talented schedulers has a knack for business but is doing manual data entry, it's your fault for not delegating correctly. If your junior trader who is sharp at making money is spending half her day creating, reviewing, distributing, and troubleshooting your daily profit and loss reports, it's your fault for not delegating properly. If your most talented software developer is working on a mundane project bandaging legacy software instead of implementing new AI projects that will help the traders make more money, you're being a bad delegator. You don't have to be a manager to delegate. If you feel a task has been delegated to you and you're not the right person for it or if it is preventing you from making money for the company, then you should let your manager know so that the task is delegated to the most suitable team member. But this should not be treated as an excuse for shirking work. Another reason for not delegating is that people may think they may be laid off or replaced by training someone else to do their task. If you're so good at a task and have mastered it, it's time to learn a new, more challenging task to increase your take-home pay. There are always new things to learn, new skills to acquire. You can't keep commanding annual pay increases for doing the same task every year. This is a recipe for obsolescence. You need to show an ability to successfully manage new challenging tasks that no one else in your company is handling today. It is also condescending to think that only you are good enough to do a task correctly, so you try to do everything yourself. This modus operandi is the exact opposite of what high earners in our industry are doing. If you're guilty of this knowingly or unknowingly, then stop! You are hurting your career and your take-home pay prospects. This is not me saying it. These are all the high earners in our industry expressing the same idea of delegation being important. But proper delegation is also an art and is not done correctly by many professionals. To help you learn this art of delegation, there are several books you can buy on Amazon.

5. They use something better than Pareto. The Pareto principle says that 80 percent of results come from 20 percent of things. In order to achieve success, your goal is to find what those 20 percent of your tasks are that produce 80 percent of your desired results. Focus your time on that 20 percent of tasks. That will give you a leverage of 16 to 1 over everybody else around you. But I want to take this a step further. Let's say you identify 20 percent of your most important tasks. Now take 20 percent of the 20 percent. That gives you a leverage of 250 to 1 over everybody else around you! If you take 20 percent of the 20 percent of the 20 percent, that gives you a leverage of 4,000 to 1!

80/20 = 16:1

64/4 = 250:1

52/0.8 = 4,000:1

40/0.2 = 65,000:1

From this, we see that 0.2 percent of the causes are creating 40 percent of your results! Let's understand this with an example. Let's say you're the commissioner of Houston, in charge of fixing the potholes in the downtown area. The problem is that there are too many roads to fix with the small budget you have at your disposal. You could fix 80 percent of citizens' pothole complaints by fixing 20 percent of the streets. But you don't have the money to fix 20 percent of the streets. So what do you do? Well, you could fix 4 percent of the streets and fix 100 percent of the complaints of 64 percent of the citizens. But maybe you don't even have that much money. If you fix less than 1 percent of the streets, you could change 100 percent of the lifestyle of 52 percent of the citizens. That's the power of leverage. The same amount of dollars applied to the right problem can have a massive impact. You just have to choose the right problem to apply your leverage to. Small hinges swing big doors. When you're going about your day trying to decide which tasks you will work on today, choose the ones that create the biggest impact on your take-home pay. Coincidentally, those will also have the biggest impact on your company's profit.

Bonus

How to Come Up with Your Money-Making Business Idea

Have you ever dreamed of quitting your job and becoming a self-made entrepreneur but felt lost on where to begin? I get asked these questions a lot: "How do I come up with a money-making idea?" "How did you get the idea to start your own software company?" A lot of people would love to quit their jobs and become self-made entrepreneurs. But they do not know what business to start. To come up with a money-making idea for a new business, here are some of the responses I got from professionals who are currently working for someone but would like to start their own business:

- Earn an MBA from a top-tier school
- Analyze market trends
- Explore online communities
- Read biographies of successful entrepreneurs
- Network with entrepreneurs
- Attend industry conferences
- Read industry reports
- Monitor patents and innovations
- Explore government grants and initiatives
- Attend pitch events

Surprisingly, the answer is none of the above! The secret to a money-making idea isn't as elusive as you might think. In this chapter, I'm going to unlock a powerful framework that will transform your frustrations and everyday observations into lucrative business ventures. This is more than just a guide; it's a blueprint to ignite your entrepreneurial spirit and turn your aspirations into reality. Get ready to dive into the thrilling world of entrepreneurship, where your next big idea is just a spark of inspiration away. Let's embark on this journey to uncover the secret of creating a successful business from scratch.

We will use the painkillers versus vitamin framework. If you were an entrepreneur, would you want to make a painkiller or a vitamin? Most entrepreneurs tend to say vitamins. That's the first mistake. A painkiller solves your problem today. If you have back pain and I offer to sell you a painkiller, you will buy it at any price. But if I sell you a vitamin with a promise that if you keep consuming these vitamins for the next ten years, then you may never suffer back pain in your old age, your answer may be, "Thanks, Jay. But I'll take the painkiller today."

There is nothing wrong with making a vitamin-type product. But it should not be your first product. Why? Because startups don't have much time to survive. According to the U.S. Bureau of Labor Statistics,[3] two out of ten new businesses fail in the first year of operations for various reasons. You want to build a painkiller-type product that people will pay money for immediately by deriving the benefit of using your product. That's a painkiller-type product, not vitamin-type.

To come up with your money-making business ideas, all you need to do is make a painkiller-type product. But there are many types of painkiller medicines. You may ask, what part of the body should the painkiller target? In order to answer this question, you

---

[3] U.S. Bureau of Labor Statistics, "Business Employment Dynamics," last modified: April 28, 2016, https://www.bls.gov/bdm/entrepreneurship/bdm_chart3.htm

need to identify a pain point. It begs the question: How do you identify a pain point?

Good news: Pain points are all around us! The next time you experience a frustration in your daily life, note it down in the Notes section of your smartphone. Here are some examples of how accidental entrepreneurs were born from identifying frustrations and pain points in their daily lives.

Uber: In December 2008, Travis Kalanick and Garrett Camp were attending the Le Web tech conference in Paris. After struggling to find a taxi on a snowy night, they began discussing the idea of a service that could easily connect passengers with drivers via a mobile app. To solve this pain point, Uber was born.

Airbnb: In October 2007, Brian Chesky and Joe Gebbia were struggling to pay the rent for their apartment in San Francisco. They noticed that a large design conference, the Industrial Designers Society of America conference, was coming to town, and all the hotels were fully booked. This gave them the idea to rent out air mattresses in their living room to conference attendees as a way to solve the pain point of not having rent money. They called their service "Air Bed & Breakfast." The rest is history.

Spanx: In 1998, Sara Blakely was getting ready for a party and wanted a smooth look under her white pants. She tried wearing traditional pantyhose but found them uncomfortable and unflattering due to the visible seams and the feet section. Out of frustration, she cut off the feet of the pantyhose, creating a makeshift solution that smoothed her silhouette while remaining more comfortable. This was the prototype for her women's undergarment product. Spanx is now a household name, and Sarah Blakely is a billionaire.

Starbucks: Howard Schultz was frustrated by the lack of a coffee culture in the United States similar to what he experienced in Italy. He saw an opportunity to create a space where people could enjoy high-quality coffee and gather socially. Schultz transformed Starbucks from a small coffee bean retailer into a global coffeehouse chain that emphasizes the customer experience.

Netflix: Reed Hastings was frustrated by the high late fees he incurred from renting a movie from Blockbuster (brick-and-mortar movie rental stores). He saw the inefficiencies and inconvenience of traditional video rental stores. He cofounded Netflix, initially offering DVD rentals by mail and later transitioning to an Internet-based streaming service that revolutionized how people consume media. Blockbuster went bankrupt.

Amazon: Jeff Bezos was so frustrated with the limitations and inefficiencies in the traditional retail model, particularly the inability to offer a vast selection of products to customers, that he founded Amazon as an online bookstore. Amazon later expanded to become the world's largest online retailer, offering a wide array of products and services.

Tesla: Musk was so frustrated by the lack of innovation in the automotive industry, particularly the slow adoption of sustainable energy solutions, that he spurred Tesla, which focuses on creating high-performance electric vehicles and advancing renewable energy technologies, pushing the industry toward a more sustainable future.

Slack: While working on a gaming software, Stewart Butterfield was so frustrated by the inefficiency of communication tools available for his team that he pivoted to create Slack, a messaging platform designed for teams and businesses to improve communication and collaboration. Slack was initially meant to be used internally only for Butterfield's own company employees. Today, every major corporation uses it.

WhatsApp: Jan Koum and Brian Acton were so frustrated with the limitations and costs of traditional SMS and text messaging services that they created WhatsApp, a messaging app that allows users to send free text messages, voice messages, images, and videos over the Internet, providing a more versatile and cost-effective communication tool. WhatsApp was acquired by Facebook and is the most popular messaging app in Asia today.

NatGasHub.com: When I showed up to JPMorgan on the first day of work, I was so frustrated at having to navigate to so many different pipeline websites every day. Out of this pain point came the idea to build one portal for all natural gas pipelines. I started my company in 2020. I am humbled to see our solution become the industry standard by 2023. I am deeply grateful to all our clients who have embraced and supported NatGasHub.com. The solution I built has become the industry standard for shippers to communicate with pipelines. Thank you for being a crucial part of this journey and for believing in the vision. Your trust and support have made all the difference. This is how I started my entrepreneurial journey. In retrospect, I wish I had experienced this frustration sooner in life! Here is a picture of me experiencing this pain point my first day on the job:

The next time you're frustrated by being stuck in traffic or the grocery line, or when you want to punch the customer service associate on the other end of the phone, note down the cause of your frustration. Treat every frustration as an opportunity. It may change your perspective on life. By transforming these frustrations into opportunities, you can create solutions that people are willing to pay for, leading to successful business ventures. Once you have ten frustrations noted down in your smartphone, rank them according to the ones that you think people will pay money to get rid of. These are your money-making pain points. Ask yourself, Which pain point are you most equipped to solve? Which one do you have a passion and the skills for? Poll friends and family to see which one of these ten they'd be willing to pay money for to make their lives frustration-free. You only need one idea to start. Keep it simple. Voilà, that is the business idea you should pursue!

Once you launch one product, you will get ideas for other related products to grow your company. I guarantee that! Now that you have identified a pain point, you can start your own company to solve this pain point. Before you know it, you may be following in the footsteps of many other accidental entrepreneurs who started just like you and went on to become billionaires!

Conclusion

As we reach the end of our journey through the intricate and dynamic world of natural gas trading, scheduling, and technology, it is essential to reflect on the key takeaways that this book has imparted. The natural gas industry is a complex yet fascinating sector that plays a critical role in our daily lives, from powering our homes to fueling our economies.

Becoming a Profitable Trader

We discussed "Ten for Ten: Ten Trading Strategies to Make You $10 Million per Year." By harnessing the power of these ten strategies, natural gas traders can aim for substantial financial success, proving that strategic trading is about not just luck but also meticulous planning and execution. The natural gas market is unique in its volatility, opportunities, and challenges. For traders, understanding the fundamental aspects of supply and demand, storage, transportation, and the various financial instruments available is paramount. The strategies and techniques discussed, from valuing and trading gas storage and transport to the ten strategies for making significant profits, offer a comprehensive guide for both novice and experienced traders. The emphasis on the three essential equations every trader must know underscores the importance of a solid foundation in the technical aspects of trading.

Mastering the Role of a Scheduler

Schedulers play a crucial role in ensuring the smooth flow of natural gas across the vast network of pipelines. The book delves into the essential nomination models and the intricacies of pipeline tariffs, providing schedulers with the knowledge they need to excel. The transition from scheduler to trader is a natural progression for those who master these skills, and the guidance provided on managing time and stress is invaluable in maintaining a balanced and productive career.

Technologists Are the Backbone of Any Natural Gas Company

The advent of AI and RPA has revolutionized the natural gas industry. Technologists who embrace these advancements can drive unprecedented efficiency and profitability. The book outlines practical applications of AI and RPA, demonstrating how these technologies can enhance decision-making, automate complex workflows, and ultimately boost the bottom line. For technologists, this is an exciting era of innovation, where the implementation of innovative solutions can distinguish you as a leader in the field.

Increase Your Take-Home Pay

We discussed "The Top Five Traits of High Earners in the Natural Gas Industry." By embracing discipline and building effective habits, you can overcome the inertia in your career. The success of high performers stems from strategic processes rather than innate talent, emphasizing the importance of cultivating good habits to achieve career growth and increased take-home pay.

Entrepreneurship in the Natural Gas Industry

For those with entrepreneurial aspirations, the framework of painkillers versus vitamins offers a practical approach to identifying and solving real-world problems. By focusing on immediate, pressing needs (painkillers), entrepreneurs can create solutions that are both impactful and profitable. The insights shared in the bonus chapter provide a roadmap for transforming frustrations and observations into lucrative business ventures.

The Path Forward

As you move forward in your career, whether as a trader, scheduler, or a technologist, remember that success in the natural gas industry requires a combination of knowledge, skill, and adaptability. The industry is constantly evolving, influenced by geopolitical events, technological advancements, and market dynamics. Staying informed, continuously learning, and being open to innovation are critical to maintaining a competitive edge.

The collective wisdom shared by the industry professionals interviewed for this book highlights the importance of collaboration and mentorship. Learning from those who have navigated the highs and lows of the industry can provide valuable insights and guidance. As you build your career, seek out mentors, share your knowledge, and contribute to the growth and success of the natural gas community.

A Final Word

The natural gas industry, with its rich history and pivotal role in the global energy landscape, offers immense opportunities for those willing to embrace its challenges and complexities. Whether you are trading on the front lines, ensuring the seamless flow of gas as a scheduler, harnessing the power of technology, or embarking on an entrepreneurial venture, the potential for success is vast.

As you continue on your journey, remember the words of Steve Jobs, a visionary who transformed multiple industries:

"Stay hungry."

Stay curious, keep pushing the boundaries, and never stop learning. The future of the natural gas industry is bright, and with the knowledge and insights gained from this book, you are well equipped to seize the opportunities that lie ahead.

Thank you for embarking on this journey with me. May your path be filled with success, innovation, and endless possibilities!

Afterword

Writing this book has been a transformative journey. When I first set out to explore the intricacies of natural gas trading, I could not have imagined the depth and complexity of the field.

Since completing the manuscript, several significant developments have occurred in the natural gas industry. Advances in artificial intelligence technology and changes in regulatory policies continue to evolve, underscoring the dynamic nature of this field. I encourage readers to stay informed about these changes and consider how they might impact the principles discussed in this book.

In reflecting on the broader implications of natural gas trading, it is clear that this field plays a crucial role in the global energy landscape. As we move toward a more sustainable future, understanding and innovating within this industry will be essential.

Thank you for joining me on this journey. I hope that this book has provided you with valuable knowledge and inspiration to explore further.

Index

311 Pipeline (s) 152, 153

A
ad valorem tax 53, 55
annual charge adjustment (ACA) 47
artificial intelligence (AI) 10
asset management agreement (AMA) 102

B
balance-of-the-month (BalMo) 61
basis spread option 74
Black-Scholes 52-53, 56, 77

C
calendar spread option (CSO) 51
cash 22-23, 60-62, 87, 98, 99, 105-106, 110, 116, 126, 130, 159
cashflow 26, 28, 35, 37
cash month 60-62
churn 48
commodity charge 47, 52, 57, 69, 71, 77, 160, 162
cost of capital 82, 84-86, 88

D
demand 18, 21, 43, 46, 52, 57, 64, 66-67, 70, 74, 79, 81-82, 87, 101-102, 113-115, 118-119, 125-126, 132, 141, 153, 159, 191
dollar value of one basis point 93
DV01 93-94

E
Elapsed prorated scheduled quantity (EPSQ) 154
electronic data interchange (EDI) 137
equation 1 29, 31, 39, 40, 44, 54, 83, 88
equation 2 40
equation 3 39
extrinsic value 52, 55-56, 60, 75, 77, 79

F
financial basis 21, 25, 28-30, 34-37, 39, 44, 54, 83, 88, 130
financial fixed price 34
firm 7, 22, 64, 65, 70, 83, 96, 101-102, 106, 133-134, 147, 152, 159-160
fixed price physical 23, 28, 39, 40, 44, 54, 83
force majeure 7
fuel charge 46-47, 52, 57, 71, 77, 162
futures 17-18, 20-23, 28, 29-31, 34-36, 39-40, 44, 54, 60, 62, 82, 83, 87-88, 90-91, 94, 98-99, 111, 124-128, 130

G
Gas Daily Daily (GDD) index 197

H
hedging transport 74
Henry Hub ix, 18, 22-24, 40, 53, 62, 124-126
high optionality 44-45, 49
high-turn 48-49, 99

I
injection charge 46
in-kind 46-47, 70-71, 150, 159
in-path 66-67
interest rate risk 90, 91, 94
interest rate swaps 90
interruptible 22, 64, 70, 83, 132, 134, 147, 159
intrinsic value 52, 55-58, 60, 75, 77, 79

L
L1D 22, 28-30, 32, 35-37, 54
loan 81-83, 86-91, 93-94, 100, 115-116
locational spread 74

M
mark-to-market (MTM) 73
meter bounce 153

N
notional value 73

O
Operational balancing agreement (OBA) 155
out-of-path 66, 67

P
painkiller 186
park 81-84, 86-88, 90-91, 93-94, 100
physical basis 25, 36, 37, 38, 39
physical index 21, 29, 36, 37, 39, 40, 44, 54, 83, 88
Predetermined allocation (PDA) 153
primary 8, 12, 51, 65, 66, 131, 135-137, 157, 160

Q
Quiz 39, 40

R
ratably 83
ratchets 56, 57
reservation 46, 64, 70, 74, 98, 106, 159, 160, 162
rho 90
robotic process automation (RPA) 10, 167
roll 44, 54, 62, 128, 157

S
scatter 49, 50
secondary 65, 80, 101
segmentation 79
spot trading 60
standard deviation 49, 51
storage 43-49, 51-58, 60-63, 74-75, 80, 83, 87, 90, 97-99, 101, 104, 127, 129, 130, 132, 154, 158, 164, 191
sunk cost 45, 64, 70, 72, 74, 98, 106, 159
swap 28, 30, 33, 35, 37, 126

T
Take-or-pay commitment 64
T-chart 26, 27, 28, 29, 33, 34, 35, 36, 37, 38, 84, 88
theta 98
transport 63, 64, 65, 67, 68, 69, 70, 72, 74, 75, 77, 79, 80, 101, 105, 106, 129, 130, 132, 133, 150, 152, 158, 160, 164, 191

V
value-at-risk (VaR) 31, 143
variable charge 159
vitamin 186
volatility 18, 20, 48, 49, 50, 51, 52, 53, 55, 56, 60, 61, 62, 77, 79, 98, 119, 124, 126, 167, 191

W
weighted average cost of gas (WACOG) 55
withdrawal charge 46

References

United States Energy Information Administration (2021)

Annual Energy Outlook 2021.

Washington, DC: U.S. Government Printing Office

United States Bureau of Labor Statistics

Made in the USA
Columbia, SC
09 July 2025

a6c530dd-e479-487b-a2b3-7b15c7b76b1dR04